A LAYMAN'S GUIDE TO THE BOOK OF REVELATION

A LAYMAN'S GUIDE TO THE BOOK OF REVELATION

REVEREND
FREDRICK A. WIERSCHKE

WESTBOW
PRESS®
A DIVISION OF THOMAS NELSON
& ZONDERVAN

WestBow Press books may be ordered through booksellers or by contacting:

WestBow Press
A Division of Thomas Nelson & Zondervan
1663 Liberty Drive
Bloomington, IN 47403
www.westbowpress.com
844-714-3454

Scripture taken from the King James Version of the Bible.

ISBN: 978-1-6642-0148-4 (sc)
ISBN: 978-1-6642-0147-7 (hc)
ISBN: 978-1-6642-0149-1 (e)

Library of Congress Control Number: 2020914789

Print information available on the last page.

WestBow Press rev. date: 08/21/2020

CONTENTS

FOREWORD

I have an intense interest in Bible prophecy, the Rapture, and the Second Coming of Christ Jesus. For years I have considered writing a book to assist others in understanding the Bible in general. After careful prayer and meditation, I have felt prompted by the Holy Spirit to put my impressions of the Book of Revelation into print.

Some may feel that my interpretations are incorrect, whereas others will find my interpretations to be enlightening. You alone must decide what you believe.

At the end of each chapter is a blank sheet of lined paper for you to write your own personal notes about that chapter if you choose.

The traditional view of the Book of Revelation says that seal 1 is broken on day 1 of the tribulation with the seventh bowl (vial) completing day 2,520. The first problem with this view is found in Revelation 11:15–19. Here, Christ is returning to the earth to set up His kingdom. The traditional view says that Christ does not return until Revelation 22.

The view that lines up scripturally is to put chapters 12–19 on top of chapters 6–11. This causes all the judgments to occur during the last half of the tribulation, not over the entire tribulation period of seven years.

Unless otherwise noted, all scripture references are taken from the King James Version, Red Letter Edition, a public domain translation. eText is available for free by eSword. For complete selection of electronic Bibles, see their website at http://www.esword.net.

I encourage the reader to not just take my word for what the scriptures contain. Have your own favorite translation available and compare what I have to say to what you yourself read. Be a good Bible student and study for yourself.

Note: Any words that may have been put in [square brackets are to help the reader better understand the previous word.]

Dictionary.com defines *revelation* as follows:

1. The act of revealing or disclosing.
2. Something revealed, especially a dramatic disclosure of something not previously known or realized.
3. A manifestation of divine will or truth.
4. A book of the Bible.

ACTUAL TIMELINE OF THE BOOK OF REVELATION

The Revelation of God the Father: Chapter 1
The Church Age: Chapters 2–3
The Prophetical Future—The Rapture Occurs: Chapter 4
The Seven-Sealed Scroll Is Opened: Chapter 5
The Judgments Are Revealed: Chapters 6:1–19:15

The seals are mentioned and opened in Revelation 6, beginning with 6:1 and running through 6:11.

The seals are opened over an extended period covering the midpoint of the tribulation to the final day of the tribulation (beginning with day 1,261 and culminating on day 2,520).

The trumpets are mentioned and blown in chapter 8, beginning with chapter 8:6, with the seventh trumpet not being blown until chapter 11:15.

The trumpets are blown over an extended period beginning with the midpoint of the tribulation to the final day of the tribulation (beginning with day 1,261 and culminating on day 2,520).

The bowls (vials) are mentioned and poured out beginning in Revelation 16:1, with the seventh bowl being poured out in 16:17–18)

The bowls (vials) are poured out over the last half of the great tribulation (beginning on day 1,261, with the final bowl being poured out on day 2,520).

To help the reader better understand this book, I have written *A Layman's Guide to the Book of Revelation.*

Always remember that scripture interprets scripture. If something is symbolic here, it was symbolic elsewhere in the Bible. The first use of a symbol generally is how God interprets that same symbol later. If a new meaning is assigned, the verse or verses following will make that clear to the reader.

CHAPTER 1

The Revelation of God the Father

The Revelation of Jesus Christ, which God gave unto him, to shew unto his servants things which must shortly come to pass; and he sent and signified *it* by his angel unto his servant John. (Rev. 1:1; emphasis added)

First, I would like to address a common misconception. Many believe that this is a revelation from Jesus only! On the contrary, Jesus was given this revelation by His Father. Jesus then passes this revelation, or unveiling, to John.

Who bare record of the word of God, and of the testimony of Jesus Christ, and of all things that he saw. (Rev. 1:2)

John confirms for the reader that he received this revelation from Jesus Christ, who originally received it from His Father.

Blessed *is* he that readeth, and they that hear the words of this prophecy, and keep those things which are written therein: for the time *is* at hand. (Rev. 1:3)

Many mistakenly believe that Revelation is the most mysterious and hard to understand book of the Bible. On the contrary, a special blessing is promised here to anyone who reads or anyone who hears the words of this prophecy. Because many people in John's time could not read or write, a scribe, priest, or someone else who could read would read scriptures out loud for the benefit of others.

John to the seven churches which are in Asia: Grace *be* unto you, and peace, from him which is, and which was, and which is to come; and from the seven Spirits which are before his throne. (Rev. 1:4)

Here, John extends his greetings to seven literal churches that existed in his time in Asia Minor, which is modern-day Turkey.

And from Jesus Christ, *who is* the faithful witness, *and* the first begotten of the dead, and the prince of the kings of the earth. Unto him that loved us, and washed us from our sins in his own blood. (Rev. 1:5)

Now, John extends greetings from Jesus Christ Himself. When John calls Jesus the "first begotten of the dead," he is acknowledging that Jesus was the first one raised to immortality—never to face physical death again!

And hath made us kings and priests unto God and his Father; to him *be* glory and dominion for ever and ever. Amen. (Rev. 1:6; emphasis added)

Through the atoning sacrifice of Jesus Christ, we believers have been made kings and priests unto Him and His Father! (In Christ, there is neither male nor female.)

There is neither Jew nor Greek, there is neither bond nor free, there is neither male nor female: for ye are all one in Christ Jesus. (Gal. 3:28)

Behold, he cometh with clouds; and every eye shall see him, and they *also* which pierced him: and all kindreds of the earth shall wail because of him. Even so, Amen. (Rev. 1:7; emphasis added)

Clouds in scripture can be symbolic. Here, believers are called clouds, foretelling the time when Jesus will return to earth in flesh, and every man, woman, and child on earth will see Him.

I am Alpha and Omega, the beginning and the ending, saith the Lord, which is, and which was, and which is to come, the Almighty. (Rev. 1:8) [Because the publisher of the King James Version colors the words of Jesus in Red, I have left this to help the reader understand, Jesus is speaking]

The Greek use the term "the Alpha and the Omega," but this is not quite accurate. This translates as the "the beginning and the end." It should be translated to "I am the Aleph and the Taw," the first and last letters of the Hebrew alphabet. Jesus is the first one to be resurrected and the last Adam.

And so it is written, The first man Adam was made a living soul; the last Adam *was made* a quickening spirit. (1 Cor. 15:45; emphasis added)

I John, who also am your brother, and companion in tribulation, and in the kingdom and patience of Jesus Christ, was in the isle that is called Patmos, for the word of God, and for the testimony of Jesus Christ. (Rev. 1:9)

John is reminding his readers that he is their brother in Christ and companion in tribulation. Remember that John had been thrown into a vat of boiling oil by the emperor Domitian. *Foxe's Book of Martyrs* lists John as having been miraculously delivered from being boiled in oil. John was then sentenced to the island Patmos until he was pardoned by the emperor Pertinax. John lived out his days in Ephesus.

I was in the Spirit on the Lord's day, and heard behind me a great voice, as of a trumpet. (Rev. 1:10)

Many debate whether this refers to Sunday or whether John was speaking prophetically at this point. I read this as John worshipping on the first day of the week, and during this time of worship, Jesus appeared to him. Notice that John described the voice of Jesus as a trumpet.

Saying, I am Alpha and Omega, the first and the last: and, What thou seest, write in a book, and send *it* unto the seven churches which are in Asia; unto Ephesus, and unto Smyrna, and unto Pergamos, and unto Thyatira, and unto Sardis, and unto Philadelphia, and unto Laodicea. (Rev. 1:11; emphasis added)

Seven is God's number of completion. The seven churches were literal churches at the time of John, and they also symbolized the stages of the church over the next couple thousand years.

And I turned to see the voice that spake with me. And being turned, I saw seven golden candlesticks. (Rev. 1:12)

Candlesticks is not an accurate translation here. John saw seven golden lamp stands. The Jews did not use candlesticks.

And in the midst of the seven candlesticks *one* like unto the Son of man, clothed with a garment down to the foot, and girt about the paps with a golden girdle. (Rev. 1:13; emphasis added)

Only those in authority in ancient times wore full-length garments and golden girdles around the chest. John describes Jesus to us as our high priest and intercessor.

His head and *his* hairs *were* white like wool, as white as snow; and his eyes *were* as a flame of fire. (Rev. 1:14; emphasis added)

His white hair and beard indicates that He is from old, as God—He is the ancient of days. This also speaks of His righteousness.

Until the Ancient of days came, and judgment was given to the saints of the most High; and the time came that the saints possessed the kingdom. (Dan. 7:22)

Christ's eyes looking like flames of fire indicate His authority to correctly judge everything He sees, and Jesus is not happy with the sin He sees in His churches.

> And his feet like unto fine brass, as if they burned in
> a furnace; and his voice as the sound of many waters.
> (Rev. 1:15)

John describes the feet of Jesus looking like fine brass. This indicates Jesus's authority as the righteous judge. When all on the earth find out later in chapters 19 and 20, His voice is unmistakable!

> And he had in his right hand seven stars: and out of
> his mouth went a sharp two-edged sword: and his
> countenance *was* as the sun shineth in his strength.
> (Rev. 1:16; emphasis added)

The stars are symbolic of the seven angels assigned to the seven churches, and the sword is symbolic of the power that proceeds out of the mouth of Jesus. His countenance was as bright as the sun, indicating the status as God that He again holds.

> And when I saw him, I fell at his feet as dead. And he laid
> his right hand upon me, saying unto me, Fear not; I am
> the first and the last. (Rev. 1:17)

John falls to Jesus's feet overwhelmed by the sight and sounds. Jesus touches John and reassures him of who He is.

> *I am* he that liveth, and was dead; and, behold, I am alive
> for evermore, Amen; and have the keys of hell and of
> death. (Rev. 1:18; emphasis added)

Jesus reminds John that He lived as a man, died, and is now alive forevermore.

> Write the things which thou hast seen, and the things
> which are, and the things which shall be hereafter. (Rev.
> 1:19)

Jesus commands John to write down the things he saw, the things that were currently happening, and the things that were to come.

The mystery of the seven stars which thou sawest in my right hand, and the seven golden candlesticks. The seven stars are the angels of the seven churches: and the seven candlesticks which thou sawest are the seven churches. (Rev. 1:20)

Jesus explains to John what the seven stars and the seven candlesticks (lamp stands) mean, leaving no doubt in John's mind or the minds of readers what is meant here.

CHAPTER 2

Letters to the First Four Churches

The Church of Ephesus: The Apostolic Church, Covering AD 30–100

This first letter must have stung the aged apostle. Church history tells us that John was the bishop (overseer) of Ephesus. He could not have been happy when Jesus pointed out the things He disapproved of. This church existed from about AD 30 (shortly after Pentecost) to about AD 100—around the natural death of John.

Because a Hebraic translation of the book of Revelation uses the word *messenger* in place of *angel*, I hold the position that this is a ministering spirit sent to the congregation at Ephesus.

In the first of seven letters, John is told to write to the church of Ephesus (the apostolic church AD 30–100).

> Unto the angel of the church of Ephesus write; These things saith he that holdeth the seven stars in his right hand, who walketh in the midst of the seven golden candlesticks. (Rev. 2:1)

In verse 2, Jesus affirms to the church of Ephesus that He is well aware of their works (their deeds), their labor (their actions in spreading the gospel), and their patience in a time of tribulation. I am sure many there were praying for the return of John and of Jesus Himself. Jesus commends them for rejecting those who claimed to be apostles and in reality were not sent by Christ.

> I know thy works, and thy labour, and thy patience, and
> how thou canst not bear them which are evil: and thou
> hast tried them which say they are apostles, and are not,
> and hast found them liars. (Rev. 2:2)

In verse 3, Jesus affirms the faithfulness of those of the Church of Ephesus. Despite being put through tribulations of their own, they held fast to the truth of the Gospel and refused to give up.

> And hast borne, and hast patience, and for my name's
> sake hast laboured, and hast not fainted. (Rev. 2:3)

Jesus commended the Ephesus church first; now He outlines that which He does not approve of.

> Nevertheless I have *somewhat* against thee, because
> thou hast left thy first love. (Rev. 2:4; emphasis added)

The Church of Ephesus was no longer in love with Him like they were in the beginning.

> Remember therefore from whence thou art fallen, and
> repent, and do the first works; or else I will come unto
> thee quickly, and will remove thy candlestick out of his
> place, except thou repent. (Rev. 2:5)

Jesus reminds them of where they had once been: probably as in love with Jesus as John himself was. For whatever reason, they lost that fervor. As a result, the church of Ephesus ceased to exist after the Mohammedan invasion around AD 712.

> But this thou hast, that thou hatest the deeds of the
> Nicolaitans, which I also hate. (Rev. 2:6)

The Nicolaitans, Greek for "Victory over the Laity," were church leaders who would not allow the congregation to think for themselves or believe what the Bible said. They demanded that members submit to their own personal interpretation of the Bible, often imposing manmade rules on the members and teaching the members that these rules were from God Himself!

Here, Jesus commends the Church of Ephesus for hating the deeds of Nicolaitans.

> He that hath an ear, let him hear what the Spirit saith unto the churches; To him that overcometh will I give to eat of the tree of life, which is in the midst of the paradise of God. (Rev. 2:7)

When Jesus says "let him who has an ear," He is saying that anyone who is willing to listen to Him or the Holy Spirit should give attention to what is being said to each of the seven churches, not just the one to which he or she belonged.

> And unto the angel of the church in Smyrna write; These things saith the first and the last, which was dead, and is alive. (Rev. 2:8)

The Church of Smyrna: The Persecuted Church, Covering AD 100–312

In the second of the seven letters, Jesus turns His attention to the Church of Smyrna.

> I know thy works, and tribulation, and poverty, (but thou art rich) and *I know* the blasphemy of them which say they are Jews, and are not, but *are* the synagogue of Satan. (Rev. 2:9; emphasis added)

Again, Jesus starts out by commending the congregation of Smyrna. He knows their work, tribulation, and poverty. Although He admits they are poor in the world's eyes, He points out that they are actually rich because they refused to conform to the world and held fast to Him! He also acknowledges that there are those who try to come in and say they are Jews but are actually of the synagogue of Satan. These were people who claimed to be circumcised in the spirit and not just of the flesh. We would call them false Christians today.

Note: Jesus does not have one word of condemnation for this church. Only the Church of Philadelphia shares this honor.

> Fear none of those things which thou shalt suffer: behold, the devil shall cast *some* of you into prison, that ye may be tried; and ye shall have tribulation ten days: be thou faithful unto death, and I will give thee a crown of life. (Rev. 2:10; emphasis added)

Here, Jesus encourages the Church of Smyrna to remain strong even though they would suffer great persecution. This church suffered under ten different Roman Emperors, beginning with Nero (circa AD 54) and ending with Diocletian (circa AD 284).

Roman Emperors

This list includes only those emperors who openly persecuted Christians.
Nero (reigned from AD 54 to 68). Under Nero, Peter was crucified and Paul was beheaded. Paul had to be beheaded because he was a born a Roman citizen, and Roman law prohibited a Roman citizen from being crucified or even flogged without being convicted in a court of Roman law. Compare this to Acts 22:24–28.

> The chief captain commanded him to be brought into the castle and bade that he should be examined by scourging; that he might know wherefore they cried so against him. And as they bound him with thongs, Paul said unto the centurion that stood by, Is it lawful for you to scourge a man that is a Roman, and uncondemned? When the centurion heard *that*, he went and told the chief captain, saying, Take heed what thou doest: for this man is a Roman. Then the chief captain came, and said unto him, Tell me, art thou a Roman? He said, Yea.
>
> And the chief captain answered, With a great sum obtained I this freedom. And Paul said, But I was *free* born. (emphasis added)

Nero was followed by the following.

Domitian (reigned from AD 81 to 96). Under Domitian, John was thrown into a vat of boiling oil and later exiled to the island of Patmos.

Trajan (reigned from AD 98 to 117). Under Trajan, Ignatius was burned at the stake.

Marcus Aurelius (reigned from AD 161 to 180).

Severus (reigned from AD 193 to 211).

Maximinius (reigned from AD 235 to 238).

Decius (reigned from AD 249 to 251).

Valerian (reigned from AD 253 to 260).

Aurelian (reigned from AD 270 to 275).

Diocletian (reigned from AD 284 to 305). Diocletian was considered the worst persecutor of Christians, as well as the worst emperor Rome ever had. Under Diocletian, many Roman cities had public burnings of the sacred Scripture texts.

The early Church father Polycarp was burned at the stake (AD 156).

> He that hath an ear, let him hear what the Spirit saith
> unto the churches; He that overcometh shall not be hurt
> of the second death. (Rev. 2:11)

Jesus encourages His Church that even if they die in this world, they will live forever with Him.

The Church of Pergamos: The Indulged Church, Covering AD 312–606

To start with, Pergamos means bigamy and polygamy. This church was a "marriage" of Christianity and the world. When Satan failed to stop the spread of the Gospel during the Smyrna era, he changed tactics and made the church and the world one.

> And to the angel of the church in Pergamos write; These things saith he which hath the sharp sword with two edges (Rev. 2:12)

Jesus points out immediately that He holds a sharp sword with two edges that can cut both ways. He can cut away anything that He does not approve of because His Father, He, and the Holy Spirit are all one. Jesus has two others to confirm a judgment against anyone or anything that is not in line with His Father's will.

> I know thy works, and where thou dwellest, *even* where Satan's seat *is:* and thou holdest fast my name, and hast not denied my faith, even in those days wherein Antipas *was* my faithful martyr, who was slain among you, where Satan dwelleth. (Rev. 2:13; emphasis added)

Here, Jesus confirms that He knows the works of the congregation of Pergamus, both good and bad. When He says He knows where they dwell, He means that He is well aware that many in Pergamos were willing to tolerate Pagan practices in order to be more acceptable to the Pagan populace.

> But I have a few things against thee, because thou hast there them that hold the doctrine of Balaam, who taught Balac to cast a stumbling block before the children of Israel, to eat things sacrificed unto idols, and to commit fornication. (Rev. 2:14)

On the one hand, some people in Pergamos had adopted a worldly view, meaning they would say that they are Christians but in reality were idol worshippers.

Remember, God used a donkey to speak to Balaam to get him to come to his senses. Balaam had been hired by Balac (Balak) to curse the nation of Israel. God instead used this opportunity to bless the people and nation of Israel.

Balaam taught his people to eat things sacrificed to idols and to commit fornication. Both sins were forbidden by God in the Mosaic law. Refer to Numbers 22:5–31:16 for the full story of Balaam.

> So hast thou also them that hold the doctrine of the Nicolaitans, which thing I hate. (Rev. 2:15)

Again, those who hold to the doctrine of "victory over the laity" were strongly rooted and accepted in Pergamus.

> Repent; or else I will come unto thee quickly and will fight against them with the sword of my mouth. (Rev. 2:16)

Jesus warns this local church that if they did not repent and return unto Him and the true Gospel, He would remove their candlestick (lamp stand) and would fight against them.

> He that hath an ear, let him hear what the Spirit saith unto the churches; To him that overcometh will I give to eat of the hidden manna, and will give him a white stone, and in the stone a new name written, which no man knoweth saving he that receiveth *it*. (Rev. 2:17; emphasis added)

Jesus encourages those who refuse to submit to these pagan doctrines. He would give them the hidden manna (the Word of God), which would fill the true believer's spirit and soul.

The Church of Thyatira: The Pagan Church, Covering AD 606 to the Tribulation

> And unto the angel of the church in Thyatira write; These things saith the Son of God, who hath his eyes like unto a flame of fire, and his feet *are* like fine brass. (Rev. 2:18, emphasis added)

Again, Jesus describes Himself in His role as Judge over those who live on the earth; especially those who claim to be His.

> I know thy works, and charity, and service, and faith, and
> thy patience, and thy works; and the last *to be* more than
> the first. (Rev. 2:19, emphasis added)

Jesus confirms that He knows the works, charity, service, faith, and patience of the Thyatirian church. Locally, the church was well-known for being a church that put action to their faith. They reached out to those in need, not just preaching the Gospel but actually living the Gospel to be a powerful witness to others.

> Notwithstanding I have a few things against thee, because
> thou sufferest that woman Jezebel, which calleth herself a
> prophetess, to teach and to seduce my servants to commit
> fornication, and to eat things sacrificed unto idols. (Rev. 2:20)

Here, I believe there was a real woman in this church who perverted the teachings of the Bible. Jesus calls her Jezebel because of her sins. She called herself a prophetess and taught true believers that it is okay to commit fornication and to even eat things sacrificed to idols.

> And I gave her space to repent of her fornication; and she
> repented not. (Rev. 2:21)

Here, Jesus tells us that He gave her time and space to repent, but she did not.

> Behold, I will cast her into a bed, and them that commit
> adultery with her into great tribulation, except they
> repent of their deeds. (Rev. 2:22)

Jesus tells us that He would cast her unto a bed of affliction, as well as all who committed adultery with her. I believe Jesus is referring to physical and spiritual adultery.

> And I will kill her children with death; and all the
> churches shall know that I am he which searcheth the
> reins and hearts: and I will give unto every one of you
> according to your works. (Rev. 2:23)

Jesus gives an ominous warning. He would kill her children, those who accepted her teachings and in turn taught others the same thing.

> But unto you I say, and unto the rest in Thyatira, as many as have not this doctrine, and which have not known the depths of Satan, as they speak; I will put upon you none other burden. (Rev. 2:24)

Now Jesus encourages those members of this congregation. He promises that because they held fast to Him, He will not add anything more onto them. He assures them that they are doing what they should in His eyes.

> But that which ye have *already* hold fast till I come. (Rev. 2:25)

He tells true believers to hold fast to what they already know and have.

> And he that overcometh, and keepeth my works unto the end, to him will I give power over the nations. (Rev. 2:26)

Here, Jesus promises those who remain faithful to Him unto to the end. He would give them power over the nations. This verse speaks of the end-time when believers (Jew and Gentile) would rule the nations.

> And he shall rule them with a rod of iron; as the vessels of a potter shall they be broken to shivers: even as I received of my Father. (Rev. 2:27)

This is a prophecy first mentioned in Psalm 2:9.
Thou shalt break them with a rod of iron; thou shalt dash them in pieces like a potter's vessel.
And again in Revelation.

> And he shall rule them with a rod of iron; as the vessels of a potter shall they be broken to shivers: even as I received of my Father. (Rev. 2:27)

And she brought forth a man child, who was to rule all nations with a rod of iron: and her child was caught up unto God, and *to* his throne. (Rev. 12:5; emphasis added)

And out of his mouth goeth a sharp sword, that with it he should smite the nations: and he shall rule them with a rod of iron: and he treadeth the winepress of the fierceness and wrath of Almighty God. (Rev. 19:15)

And I will give him the morning star. (Rev. 2:28)

Here, God the Father has given Jesus "the morning star." In turn, Jesus grants true believers the right to "rule and reign with Him for one thousand years."

And I saw thrones, and they sat upon them, and judgment was given unto them: and *I saw* the souls of them that were beheaded for the witness of Jesus, and for the word of God, and which had not worshipped the beast, neither his image, neither had received *his* mark upon their foreheads, or in their hands; and they lived and reigned with Christ a thousand years. (Rev. 20:4; emphasis added)

In addition, we will share in a glorious time of perfection! Jesus will have all authority over all the earth and will enforce His peace. In addition, we will have His presence not only for the one thousand years but for eternity!

He that hath an ear, let him hear what the Spirit saith unto the churches. (Rev. 2:29)

Jesus is calling everyone to return unto Him so all faithful believers will not miss out on any rewards that He will give out at the judgment seat of Christ.

CHAPTER 3

Letters to the Last Three Churches

The Church of Sardis: The Dead Church, Covering AD 1520 to the Tribulation

[The Protestant Reformation]

> And unto the angel of the church in Sardis write; These things saith he that hath the seven Spirits of God, and the seven stars; I know thy works, that thou hast a name that thou livest, and art dead. (Rev. 3:1)

Jesus exposes the Church of Sardis as being a "paper tiger." In certain communities around the church, they were thought to be an alive church. Jesus points out that they are actually dead in His eyes.

> Be watchful, and strengthen the things which remain, that are ready to die: for I have not found thy works perfect before God. (Rev. 3:2)

This admonition is for the majority of the church members who formed this congregation. Note later in Revelation 3:4 that Jesus commends some of the congregation.

> Remember therefore how thou hast received and heard, and hold fast, and repent. If therefore thou shalt not watch, I will come on thee as a thief, and thou shalt not know what hour I will come upon thee. (Rev. 3:3)

Thou hast a few names even in Sardis which have not defiled their garments; and they shall walk with me in white: for they are worthy. (Rev. 3:4)

Though a majority of the congregation is spiritually dead, Jesus assures some of the members that He sees redeeming qualities in some.

He that overcometh, the same shall be clothed in white raiment; and I will not blot out his name out of the book of life, but I will confess his name before my Father, and before his angels. (Rev. 3:5)

To all who remain faithful unto the end, Jesus promises they will be clothed in white raiment (garments), signifying they are among the redeemed of the Lord and will hold a position of authority in His kingdom.

He that hath an ear, let him hear what the Spirit saith unto the churches. (Rev. 3:6)

Jesus once again calls everyone to come unto Him, repent of any old ways and thoughts, and be approved by Him.

The Church of Philadelphia: The Church Christ Loved, Covering AD 1750 to the Rapture

The Church of Philadelphia was well-known for its missionary stance. They sought readily to spread the gospel wherever they could.

And to the angel of the church in Philadelphia write; These things saith he that is holy, he that is true, he that hath the key of David, he that openeth, and no man shutteth; and shutteth, and no man openeth. (Rev. 3:7)

This is confirmed when Jesus says that what He opens, no man can shut. But what He does shut, no man can open.

I know thy works: behold, I have set before thee an open door, and no man can shut it: for thou hast a little strength, and hast kept my word, and hast not denied my name. (Rev. 3:8)

The local church members have little strength in and of themselves. With Jesus on their side, they have all the strength they need.

Behold, I will make them of the synagogue of Satan, which say they are Jews, and are not, but do lie; behold, I will make them to come and worship before thy feet, and to know that I have loved thee. (Rev. 3:9)

Although Jesus uses the term *synagogue*, there is nothing wrong with reading it as congregation or even a local church. Here, he is comparing those who outwardly claim to be believers but inside do not know Jesus Christ as their own personal Lord and Savior.

Because thou hast kept the word of my patience, I also will keep thee from the hour of temptation, which shall come upon all the world, to try them that dwell upon the earth. (Rev. 3:10)

I am among those who hold that this verse is the Lord's promise to remove the Philadelphia Church at the time of the Rapture.

Behold, I come quickly: hold that fast which thou hast, that no man take thy crown. (Rev. 3:11)

Jesus is reminding His Church that He is coming quickly and that they should remain faithful and steadfast so they do not lose any rewards they have already earned. For more information on the Rapture and my interpretation of the scriptures, read chapter 4 of this book.

Him that overcometh will I make a pillar in the temple of my God, and he shall go no more out: and I will write upon him the name of my God, and the name of the city of my God, *which is* new Jerusalem, which cometh down

out of heaven from my God: and *I will write upon him
my new name.* (Rev. 3:12; emphasis added)

When Christ says He will make a believer "a pillar in the temple of my God," He is commending that believer for being steadfast and faithful, one who is not shaken in one's faith no matter what the enemy has thrown at the believer.

He that hath an ear, let him hear what the Spirit saith
unto the churches. (Rev. 3:13)

Notice Jesus did not have one word of condemnation for this church. Only commendation or praise! Only the Church of Smyrna also received this status for their faithfulness. We should learn from these two churches and press forward to receive the prize Christ has waiting for us.

The Church of Laodecia, the Lukewarm Church, Covering AD 1900 to the End of the Tribulation

And unto the angel of the church of the Laodiceans
write; These things saith the Amen, the faithful and
true witness, the beginning of the creation of God. (Rev.
3:14)

Jesus reminds the Laodiceans just who He is and how He fits into the process of creation.

I know thy works, that thou art neither cold nor hot: I
would thou wert cold or hot. (Rev. 3:15)

Sadly, Jesus has no words of praise for this church, only Condemnation. Of the seven churches, two got praise and no condemnation, four got both praise and condemnation, and one got no praise at all.

So then because thou art lukewarm, and neither cold nor
hot, I will spue thee out of my mouth. (Rev. 3:16)

Jesus gives them a stern warning because they are neither hot nor cold. He will spit (spew) them out of His mouth. Just as we would spit out a mouthful of lukewarm water, so would He spit them out.

> Because thou sayest, I am rich, and increased with goods, and have need of nothing; and knowest not that thou art wretched, and miserable, and poor, and blind, and naked. (Rev. 3:17)

Sadly, the Laodicean church brags that they are rich and increased with goods. Financially and materially, they were blessed in abundance. But they had absolutely forgotten the very Lord and Savior who gave Himself for them.

> I counsel thee to buy of me gold tried in the fire, that thou mayest be rich; and white raiment, that thou mayest be clothed, and *that* the shame of thy nakedness do not appear; and anoint thine eyes with eyesalve, that thou mayest see. (Rev. 3:18; emphasis added)

Jesus sets out to remind them to purchase gold tried in the fire; this probably refers back to what Peter said in his first epistle.

> That the trial of your faith, being much more precious than of gold that perisheth, though it be tried with fire, might be found unto praise and honour and glory at the appearing of Jesus Christ. (1 Pet. 1:7)

The white raiments are a symbol of the cleanliness of the sacrifice of Jesus Christ for all who would believe. The eye salve Jesus refers to here is a spiritual one that can be obtained only from the Holy Spirit.

> As many as I love, I rebuke and chasten: be zealous therefore, and repent. (Rev. 3:19)

Though we don't like being rebuked, Christ reminds us that His motivation for rebuking us is because He loves us, and He gives us warning when we do or say something contrary to His will. He then reminds the Laodecians to turn their attention to Him and use their energy for His will.

> Behold, I stand at the door, and knock: if any man hear
> my voice, and open the door, I will come in to him, and
> will sup with him, and he with me. (Rev. 3:20)

In a famous painting by Holman Hunt, Jesus is standing outside of a closed door and gently knocks on the door. If one looks closely at the door, one notices that it does not have a doorknob on the outside!

> To him that overcometh will I grant to sit with me in my
> throne, even as I also overcame, and am set down with
> my Father in his throne. (Rev. 3:21)

Jesus seeks to encourage the Laodecians that if they remain faithful to Him, they will ultimately have rewards in heaven, just as He did when He overcame the world and sat down with His Father.

> He that hath an ear, let him hear what the Spirit saith
> unto the churches. (Rev. 3:22)

Again, Jesus is reminding believers to be doers of His Word, not just hearing and forgetting.

CHAPTER 4

The Church and What Is Coming

Chapter 4 in the Book of Revelation contains one of the most controversial doctrines in the Christian Church today: the rapture of the Church (or the Bride of Christ).

If there is no rapture, then believers stand condemned along with unbelievers.

Chapter 4 starts out with the Apostle John seeing a door that had been opened in heaven. The first question I have is, "Why, was there a door opened for just one man?" If those who oppose the view of the rapture are correct, then why did John see a door having just been opened? An open door is an invitation. An invitation for whom?

In the first verse, it appears to me that three events occur. First, John says he looked and saw a "door having been opened in the heaven." Second, he says, "The first voice, I heard was like a trumpet speaking with me, saying ..." Third, he says, "Come up here and I shall show you what has to take place after this." After this?

Compare this last event in verse 1 to Revelation 1:1, "Revelation of the Christ Jesus which God the Father gave Him [Jesus] to show His servant what has to take place with speed."

I believe that John saw a door open because the voice John heard in Revelation 4:1 was Jesus Christ Himself, calling His Bride.

Remember, Jesus said in John 10:27, "My sheep hear my voice, and I know them, and they follow me."

Because John was the only one at that time to see a future event, he was the only one brought into heaven. Compare this with Revelation 11:12, when the two witnesses have already been resurrected and are called back into heaven.

And they heard a great voice from heaven saying unto
them, Come up hither. And they ascended up to heaven
in a cloud; and their enemies beheld them. (Rev. 11:12)

From this verse, we are led to conclude that the whole world not only
sees the two witnesses ascend into heaven but also hears the voice of
Christ calling them!

I personally believe that there will be a rapture of the Church before
the tribulation begins for the following reasons.

On Earth, when one nation prepares to go war with another nation,
the aggressor nation recalls all of its ambassadors to the invaded nation.

Now then we are ambassadors for Christ, as though God
did beseech *you* by us: we pray *you* in Christ's stead, be
ye reconciled to God. (2 Cor. 5:20; emphasis added)

God has promised to reward obedience and punish disobedience. If
there is no rapture of the Church, then God the Father did something
impossible for Him to do: He lied. The Bible clearly indicates that Christ
died to pay the penalty for all our sins.

But God proves His love for us, in that while we were still
sinners, Christ died for us. (Rom. 5:5)

That whosoever believeth in him should not perish but
have eternal life. For God so loved the world, that he
gave his only begotten Son, that whosoever believeth in
him should not perish, but have everlasting life. For God
sent not his Son into the world to condemn the world;
but that the world through him might be saved. (John
3:15–17)

One must look at other names for the great tribulation: The seventieth
week of Daniel or the time of Jacob's trouble. Both expressions describe
a Jewish people, not the believing Church (both Jew and Gentile).

Seventy weeks are determined upon thy people and upon
thy holy city, to finish the transgression, and to make an

end of sins, and to make reconciliation for iniquity, and to bring in everlasting righteousness, and to seal up the vision and prophecy, and to anoint the most Holy. (Dan. 9:24)

I am among those who believe the first sixty-nine weeks were fulfilled when Jesus was crucified. Prophetically, a week is representative of a seven-year period of time.

Seventy weeks are determined upon thy people and upon thy holy city, to finish the transgression, and to make an end of sins, and to make reconciliation for iniquity, and to bring in everlasting righteousness, and to seal up the vision and prophecy, and to anoint the most Holy. Know therefore and understand, *that* from the going forth of the *commandment to restore and to build Jerusalem* unto the Messiah the Prince *shall be* seven weeks, and threescore and two weeks: the street shall be built again, and the wall, even in troublous times. (Dan. 9:24–25; emphasis added)

Now, there were a total of three decrees issued by Persian kings. The first was issued in 536 BC by Cyrus in fulfillment of a prophecy by Isaiah two hundred years earlier in which God calls Cyrus by name!

That saith of Cyrus, *He is* my shepherd, and shall perform all my pleasure: even saying to Jerusalem, Thou shalt be built; and to the temple, Thy foundation shall be laid. (Isa. 44:28; emphasis added)

Thus saith the LORD to his anointed, to Cyrus, whose right hand I have holden, to subdue nations before him; and I will loose the loins of kings, to open before him the two leaved gates; and the gates shall not be shut. (Isa. 45:1; emphasis added)

Notice in Isaiah 44:28, God says that Cyrus will order that the city be rebuilt seventy-nine years before the second edict issued in 457 BC by Darius I (aka Darius the Mede) and given to Ezra, and the third edict was given to Nehemiah by Artaxerxes I in 444 BC. Because Daniel is told there would be 1 seven (or 49 years) and then 62 sevens (434 years), I believe that using the original date of 536 BC is extremely plausible. There is an indeterminate gap between the first seven and the sixty-two sevens. A gap of seventy-nine years is not out of line. Notice we are told the streets would be rebuilt first! Streets do not threaten; enemies' walls do. Streets offer convenience in travel. Then Daniel is told that the wall would be rebuilt in troublesome times. Remember, Nehemiah faced heavy opposition when trying to rebuild the wall around Jerusalem!

Chart 4.1. Seventy Weeks of Daniel Diagramed.

-Seventy weeks are determined upon thy people and upon thy holy city, to finish the transgression, and to make an end of sins, and to make reconciliation for iniquity, and to bring in everlasting righteousness, and to seal up the vision and prophecy, and to anoint the most Holy. Know therefore and understand, *that from the going forth of the commandment to restore and to build Jerusalem unto the Messiah the Prince shall be seven weeks, and threescore and two weeks*: the street shall be built again, and the wall, even in troublous times.

And after threescore and two weeks shall Messiah be cut off, but not for himself: and the people of the prince that shall come shall destroy the city and the sanctuary; and the end thereof *shall be* with a flood, and unto the end of the war desolations are determined. (Dan. 9:24–26; [emphasis added]

In 457 BC, allowing seven sevens (49 years) and sixty-two sevens (434 years), we come up with a total of 483 years: -457 + 483 = 26.

By that calculation, we are still four years short of Jesus being about thirty years old. However, if we accept that Jesus was born in 4 BC, then the equation looks like the following.

Presuming that the original edict Daniel spoke of was issued in 457 BC and that Jesus was actually born in 4 BC, that leaves a total of thirty years, which matches the age Luke tells us Jesus began His ministry.

If the edict is issued in 457 BC, if Jesus is actually born in 4 BC, and if we allow another thirty-three years before he is crucified, we come up with the following: -457 + 453 = -4. Then if 33 years is added to 4 BC we come up with a date of AD 29, the earliest date which Jesus could have been crucified, with AD 34 being the latest date.

> And a letter unto Asaph the keeper of the king's forest, that he may give me timber to make beams for the gates of the palace which *appertained* to the house, and for the wall of the city, and for the house that I shall enter into. And the king granted me, according to the good hand of my God upon me. (Neh. 2:8; emphasis added)

Because scripture clearly indicates there is a break in the prophetic calendar, with the break, we are not to calculate the first sixty-nine weeks together. If this is done, then Jesus should have been born in 7 BC in order to have been about thirty-three when he was crucified (cut off). I believe he was born in 4 BC, and if one accepts the timeframe of the sixty-two sevens mentioned by Daniel as beginning in 536 BC and subtracts a total of 483 prophetic years from this, one comes up with the date of AD 26. This still leaves us short by four to seven years, again allow an indeterminate gap between the first seven (49 years) and the sixty-two sevens (434 years). Then according to the Gospel of Luke, Jesus was about thirty years old when he began his ministry.

> And Jesus himself began to be about thirty years of age, being (as was supposed) the son of Joseph, which was *the son* of Heli. (Luke 3:23; emphasis added)

If we accept that Jesus was about thirty-three and a half years old when he was crucified (cut off), then we find we must go back and correct our original timeline. See Chart 4.1 for more detail. However, if we accept the beginning date as 457 BC and place the birth of Jesus at 4 BC (to correct a miscalculation), then it is -457 plus 483 (69 times 7), and we come up with the year AD 30—the age Jesus should have been when he began His public ministry.

> And after threescore and two weeks shall Messiah be cut off, but not for himself: and the people of the prince that shall come shall destroy the city and the sanctuary; and the end thereof *shall be* with a flood, and unto the end of the war desolations are determined. (Dan. 9:26; emphasis added)

Here, the first sixty-nine weeks are fulfilled while the seventieth week remains. This comes from Jeremiah 30:7.

> Alas! for that day *is* great, so that none *is* like it: it *is* even the time of Jacob's trouble; but he shall be saved out of it. (emphasis added)

> How awful that day will be! No other will be like it. It will be a time of trouble for Jacob, but he will be saved out of it. (NIV)

More and more Jews are beginning to accept Jesus as the promised Messiah (*Christ* in Greek). This great revival among the Jews will occur during the seventieth week of Daniel, or the time of Jacob's trouble (Jer. 30:7).

> For the wages of sin *is* death; but the gift of God *is* eternal life through Jesus Christ our Lord. (Rom. 6:23; (emphasis added))

> For the Lord himself shall descend from heaven with a shout, with the voice of the archangel, and with the trump of God: and the dead in Christ shall rise first:

Then we which are alive *and* remain shall be caught up together with them in the clouds, to meet the Lord in the air: and so shall we ever be with the Lord. (emphasis added)

Notice Paul tells us that the dead in Christ arise first. Then we who are still alive are transformed in the twinkling of an eye (1/300 of a second). See 1 Corinthians 15:51–54.

Behold, I shew you a mystery; We shall not all sleep, but we shall all be changed, In a moment, in the twinkling of an eye, at the last trump: for the trumpet shall sound, and the dead shall be raised incorruptible, and we shall be changed. For this corruptible must put on incorruption, and this mortal *must* put on immortality. So when this corruptible shall have put on incorruption, and this mortal shall have put on immortality, then shall be brought to pass the saying that is written, Death is swallowed up in victory. (emphasis added)

See also 1 Corinthians 15:3–8.

For I delivered unto you first of all that which I also received, how that Christ died for our sins according to the scriptures; And that he was buried, and that he rose again the third day according to the scriptures: And that he was seen of Cephas [Hebrew for Peter], then of the twelve: After that, he was seen of above five hundred brethren at once; of whom the greater part remain unto this present, but some are fallen asleep. After that, he was seen of James; then of all the apostles. And last of all he was seen of me also, as of one born out of due time.

And in 1 Thessalonians 5:1–5.

But of the times and the seasons, brethren, ye have no need that I write unto you. For yourselves know perfectly that the day of the Lord so cometh as a thief in the night.

For when they shall say, Peace and safety; then sudden destruction cometh upon them, as travail upon a woman with child; and they shall not escape. But ye, brethren, are not in darkness, that that day should overtake you as a thief. Ye are all the children of light, and the children of the day: we are not of the night, nor of darkness.

Further, Paul says in 2 Thessalonians 2:1–3,

Now we beseech you, brethren, by the coming of our Lord Jesus Christ, and *by* our gathering together unto him, That ye be not soon shaken in mind, or be troubled, neither by spirit, nor by word, nor by letter as from us, as that the day of Christ is at hand. Let no man deceive you by any means: for *that day shall not come,* except there come a falling away first, and that man of sin be revealed, the son of perdition. (emphasis added)

Now, 2 Thessalonians 2:3 has caused much debate among Christian scholars. Notice that Paul clearly states that the man of lawlessness (the antichrist) appears to the world after a falling away that comes first. Many believe that this refers to many in the Church (the Body of Christ) abandoning the faith (belief in Jesus Christ) and turning to doctrines of demons (false teachings). Some hold that believers will pull away from churches that adopt these false teachings. I tend to believe in the latter. The Church will welcome nonbiblical teaching in order to fill the pews and will blatantly accept false doctrines, and they will fall away, leaving true believers to choose for themselves whether they will follow the pastor who is following Christ or the pastor who follows the antichrist.

Sadly, it will be easier for the churches to force true believers to change their home church in order to remain faithful to Christ Jesus and all of His teachings. With the advent of so-called atheist megachurches, [while atheists do not believe in an all powerful being. They have gathered together in what they call Atheist Churches]. I believe that we are about to see the fulfillment of Paul's prophecy in 2 Thessalonians 2:3. As these atheist churches continue to promulgate, they will spread a doctrine of demons, causing many true believers to pull away from any church that does not to the true Bible message.

The world stands judged starting in Revelation 6 and going through Revelation 18. The word *church* or *churches* is not found in any of these chapters. Why? Because the Church was raptured at the beginning of Revelation 4. The door that was opened in chapter 4 will not be opened again until 19:11–16; at that time, the Bride of Christ returns with Christ Himself for the end of the great tribulation. Note that Christ is the only one who does battle at the Battle of Armageddon. Believers are present but do not participate in the battle itself.

Back to the scene in heaven. John sees twenty-four elders around the throne of God. Who are the twenty-four elders? I believe they are the twelve sons of Jacob and the eleven surviving apostles—and the apostle Paul! Twelve from each the Old and New Testaments!

In 1 Peter 2:9–10 we read,

> But you are a chosen race, a royal priesthood, a set-apart nation, a people for a possession, that you should proclaim the praises of Him who called you out of darkness into His marvellous light, who once were not a people, but now the people of Elohim; who had not obtained compassion, but now obtained compassion.

As believers, we are kings and queens. The Hebrew uses the word *sovereigns*. We are also called priests. Priests belong to a specific priestly order; see 1 Chronicles 24:7–19 and Chart 4.2. This leads me to believe that each and every believer will be assigned to a priestly order, and we will serve with Him after He overthrows the kingdoms of the world and Satan for one thousand years.

See Chart 4.2 for the names and orders of the priests.

Chart 4.2. Twenty-four orders of priests, taken from 1 Chronicles 24:7–19.

Order and Name Defined

Now the first lot came forth to Jehoiarib,	"Whom Jehovah Defends"
the second to Jedaiah,	"Praise Jehovah"
The third to Harim,	"Flat-nosed"
the fourth to Seorim,	"Barley"
The fifth to Malchijah,	*Meaning unknown*
the sixth to Mijamin,	"From the Right Hand"
The seventh to Hakkoz,	"Thorn"
the eighth to Abijah,	"My Father Is Jehovah"
The ninth to Jeshua,	"Whom Jehovah Helps" or "Savior"
the tenth to Shecaniah,	"Dweller with Jehovah"
The eleventh to Eliashib,	"Whom God Restores"
the twelfth to Jakim,	"Whom God Sets Up"
The thirteenth to Huppah,	"Protected"
the fourteenth to Jeshebeab,	"Father's Seat"
The fifteenth to Bilgah,	"First-Born" or "Dispersion"; also called Aphses
the sixteenth to Immer,	"Talkative"
The seventeenth to Hezir,	"Swine"
the eighteenth to Aphses,	*Meaning unknown*
The nineteenth to Pethahiah,	"The Lord Opening or Gate of the Lord"
the twentieth to Jehezekel,	"Whom God Makes Strong"
The one and twentieth to Jachin,	"He That Strengthens and Makes Steadfast"
the two and twentieth to Gamul,	"A Recompense"
The three and twentieth to Delaiah,	"The Poor of the Lord"
the four and twentieth to Maaziah.	"Consolation of Jehovah"

And immediately I was in the spirit: and, behold, a throne was set in heaven, and *one* sat on the throne. And he that sat was to look upon like a jasper and a sardine stone: and *there was* a rainbow round about the throne, in sight like unto an emerald. And round about the throne *were* four and twenty seats: and upon the seats I saw four and twenty elders sitting, clothed in white raiment; and they had on their heads crowns of gold. (Rev. 4:2–4; emphasis added)

I believe the elders are the twelve sons of Jacob and the twelve apostles. Even though Paul was not an original apostle, I believe he is the twelfth apostle and the twenty-fourth elder!

Now that John is in the third heaven, he sees an extraordinary vision. He sees a vision of God Himself while his vision is obscured by the glory of the seven spirits of God the Father. John is able to determine that someone is seated on the heavenly throne and that someone is appearing like a jasper stone and a ruby stone and is encircled by an emerald rainbow and surrounded by twenty-four elders.

The ruby (sardine) stone is red in color, the color of fire. The jasper stone is clear in color. The first indicates that Christ will judge with fire because the rainbow reminds Him of the promise made to Noah in Genesis 9:12–13. The jasper, being clear, is to remind God all is clear before Him. Christ removed the taint of sin, so we could stand with Him before the Father.

And God said, This *is* the token of the covenant which I make between me and you and every living creature that *is* with you, for perpetual generations: I do set my bow in the cloud, and it shall be for a token of a covenant between me and the earth. (Gen. 9:12–13)

Jesus is standing next to the one seated on this throne. Remember what God told Moses in Exodus 33:20–23.

And he said, Thou canst not see my face: for there shall no man see me, and live. And the LORD said, Behold, *there is* a place by me, and thou shalt stand upon a rock:

> And it shall come to pass, while my glory passeth by, that
> I will put thee in a clift of the rock, and will cover thee
> with my hand while I pass by: And I will take away mine
> hand, and thou shalt see my back parts: but my face shall
> not be seen. (emphasis added)

But we are able to see Jesus!

Because John uses the term *elders*, they are obviously human! Also, these elders are wearing crowns, which they take off and throw before God the Father, and they are clothed in white raiment.

A spirit does not need any form of a garment. Humans would. The twenty-four elders lead all humans who have been raptured in a glorious worshipping of the Lamb of God. Also, because John sees the elders throwing their crowns before Jesus, this leads me to believe that the judgment seat of Christ is already done, and believers now have their reward (crowns) to throw before Him. Remember that Jesus is the King of kings, and we are priests and kings and queens under Him. His crown will be a very distinctive crown that only He wears. The rest of us who have been awarded crowns will wear other crowns that at a glance tell someone how many of a given crown we have earned, and which crown!

When I was in the US Air Force, we wore a ribbon on our dress jackets to indicate that we had been awarded a particular medal. If more than one of that particular medal had been awarded, we wore a bronze oak leaf cluster (some medals used different indicators) for each successive medal awarded, up to five total. The ribbon itself counted as one occurrence, and four oak leaf clusters on the ribbon told a viewer the wearer had received that medal a total of five times. I believe that a particular jewel will be set in our crown for each additional time that crown is awarded. Multiple crowns for different awards may be represented by a style or other design.

> And out of the throne proceeded lightnings and
> thunderings and voices: and *there were* seven lamps
> of fire burning before the throne, which are the seven
> Spirits of God. (Rev. 4:5; emphasis added)

In this verse tells us what comes out of the Throne! Jesus is Righteously mad! The Lightnings, thunders, and voices indicate that Judgments are about to occur on Earth!

> And before the throne *there was* a sea of glass like unto crystal: and in the midst of the throne, and round about the throne, *were* four beasts full of eyes before and behind. (Rev. 4:6)

The sea of glass before the throne indicates that all is calm in heaven. The Church is no longer on Earth and is peacefully worshipping the Lamb of God!

Next, John sees four living creatures; some translations use the term *beasts*. The latter is an incorrect translation. These creatures are not hideous monsters but very beautiful creations of God!

> And the first beast *was* like a lion, and the second beast like a calf, and the third beast had a face as a man, and the fourth beast *was* like a flying eagle. And the four beasts had each of them six wings about *him;* and *they were* full of eyes within: and they rest not day and night, saying, Holy, holy, holy, Lord God Almighty, which was, and is, and is to come. (Rev. 4:7–8; emphasis added)

Here, John is using symbolism to depict four aspects of Christ's character. Always take something in Revelation as literal unless the Bible makes clear it is making a symbolic representation. Terms such as "like a" or "as a" help tell the reader the following is to be taken figuratively. Here, John sees four aspects of Christ. Each aspect showing a different view of Christ's leadership.

> The Lion represents Christ as King (the Gospel of Matthew)

> The Calf represents Christ as the Servant (the Gospel of Mark)

> The Man represents Christ in His humanity (the Gospel of Luke)

The Eagle represents Christ in His capacity as God (the Gospel of John)

And when those beasts give glory and honour and thanks to him that sat on the throne, who liveth for ever and ever, The four and twenty elders fall down before him that sat on the throne, and worship him that liveth for ever and ever, and cast their crowns before the throne, saying, Thou art worthy, O Lord, to receive glory and honour and power: for thou hast created all things, and for thy pleasure they are and were created. (Rev. 4:9–11)

In the previous three verses, we see that the elders and the four living creatures all bow down and praise Jesus! Not only that, but all give thanks to Jesus for creating them.

CHAPTER 5

The Seven-Sealed Scroll

> And I saw in the right hand of him that sat on the throne
> a book written within and on the backside, sealed with
> seven seals. (Rev. 5:1)

The first misnomer that I want to dispel is about the Scroll and its Seven Seals. Many readers of the Book of Revelation believe it has Seven Seals on the outside of the Scroll. On the contrary! The scroll has only one Seal on the outside, after the first Seal is broken, a portion of the scroll is opened, and its contents are revealed to John. Then the scroll is rolled out until the 2nd Seal comes into view. Christ then breaks the 2nd Seal and repeats the process until ALL seven seals have been broken or opened.

> And I saw a strong angel proclaiming with a loud voice,
> Who is worthy to open the book, and to loose the seals
> thereof? (Rev. 5:2)

John weeps when he hears an angel proclaim with a loud voice, "Who is worthy to open the scroll and to loosen its seals?"
Notice the next verse tells us that no one in the heaven or on the earth was able to open and read the scroll.

> And no man in heaven, nor in earth, neither under the
> earth, was able to open the book, neither to look thereon.
> And I wept much, because no man was found worthy
> to open and to read the book, neither to look thereon.
> (Rev. 5:3–4)

Initially, John does not believe that anyone could open the scroll. In the next verse he finds out otherwise.

An Elder comforts John by telling him not to weep.

> And one of the elders saith unto me, Weep not: behold, the Lion of the tribe of Juda, the Root of David, hath prevailed to open the book, and to loose the seven seals thereof. (Rev. 5:5)

To help clarify Revelation 5:5; we need to look back at Jeremiah 32:6–17.

> And Jeremiah said, The word of the LORD came unto me, saying, Behold, Hanameel the son of Shallum thine uncle shall come unto thee, saying, Buy thee my field that *is* in Anathoth: for the right of redemption *is* thine to buy *it.* So Hanameel mine uncle's son came to me in the court of the prison according to the word of the LORD, and said unto me, Buy my field, I pray thee, that *is* in Anathoth, which *is* in the country of Benjamin: for the right of inheritance *is* thine, and the redemption *is* thine; buy *it* for thyself. Then I knew that this *was* the word of the LORD. And I bought the field of Hanameel my uncle's son, that *was* in Anathoth, and weighed him the money, *even* seventeen shekels of silver. And I subscribed the evidence, and sealed *it,* and took witnesses, and weighed *him* the money in the balances. So I took the evidence of the purchase, *both* that which was sealed *according* to the law and custom, and that which was open: And I gave the evidence of the purchase unto Baruch the son of Neriah, the son of Maaseiah, in the sight of Hanameel mine uncle's *son,* and in the presence of the witnesses that subscribed the book of the purchase, before all the Jews that sat in the court of the prison. And I charged Baruch before them, saying, Thus saith the LORD of hosts, the God of Israel; Take these evidences, this evidence of the purchase, both which is sealed, and this

evidence which is open; and put them in an earthen vessel, that they may continue many days. For thus saith the LORD of hosts, the God of Israel; Houses and fields and vineyards shall be possessed again in this land. Now when I had delivered the evidence of the purchase unto Baruch the son of Neriah, I prayed unto the LORD, saying, Ah Lord GOD! behold, thou hast made the heaven and the earth by thy great power and stretched out arm, *and* there is nothing too hard for thee. (emphasis added)

For the Jews, a scroll proving the rightful ownership of land was first sealed with seven seals. Next, the kinsman redeemer had to be able to prove ancestry gave him the right of redemption. In Jeremiah's case, a direct descendent of his would later be able prove he had the proper lineage to obtain the sealed scroll and open it.

Jesus shows His human lineage in Luke 3:23–38.

And Jesus himself began to be about thirty years of age, being (as was supposed) the son of Joseph, which was *the son* of Heli,

Which was *the son* of Matthat, which was *the son* of Levi, which was *the son* of Melchi, which was *the son* of Janna, which was *the son* of Joseph,

Which was *the son* of Mattathias, which was *the son* of Amos, which was *the son* of Naum, which was *the son* of Esli, which was *the son* of Nagge,

Which was *the son* of Maath, which was *the son* of Mattathias, which was *the son* of Semei, which was *the son* of Joseph, which was *the son* of Juda,

Which was *the son* of Joanna, which was *the son* of Rhesa, which was *the son* of Zorobabel, which was *the son* of Salathiel, which was *the son* of Neri,

Which was *the son* of Melchi, which was *the son* of Addi, which was *the son* of Cosam, which was *the son* of Elmodam, which was *the son* of Er,

Which was *the son* of Jose, which was *the son* of Eliezer, which was *the son* of Jorim, which was *the son* of Matthat, which was *the son* of Levi,

Which was *the son* of Simeon, which was *the son* of Juda, which was *the son* of Joseph, which was *the son* of Jonan, which was *the son* of Eliakim,

Which was *the son* of Melea, which was *the son* of Menan, which was *the son* of Mattatha, which was *the son* of Nathan, which was *the son* of David,

Which was *the son* of Jesse, which was *the son* of Obed, which was *the son* of Booz, which was *the son* of Salmon, which was *the son* of Naasson,

Which was *the son* of Aminadab, which was *the son* of Aram, which was *the son* of Esrom, which was *the son* of Phares, which was *the son* of Juda,

Which was *the son* of Jacob, which was *the son* of Isaac, which was *the son* of Abraham, which was *the son* of Thara, which was *the son* of Nachor,

Which was *the son* of Saruch, which was *the son* of Ragau, which was *the son* of Phalec, which was *the son* of Heber, which was *the son* of Sala,

Which was *the son* of Cainan, which was *the son* of Arphaxad, which was *the son* of Sem, which was *the son* of Noe, which was *the son* of Lamech,

Which was *the son* of Mathusala, which was *the son* of Enoch, which was *the son* of Jared, which was *the son* of Maleleel, which was *the son* of Cainan,

Which was *the son* of Enos, which was *the son* of Seth, which was *the son* of Adam, which was *the son* of God. (emphasis added)

And I looked and saw in the midst of the throne and of the four living creatures, and in the midst of the elders a Lamb standing, as having been slain, having seven horns and seven eyes, which are the seven Spirits of Elohim sent out into all the earth. (Rev. 5:6)

Here, John sees two distinct individuals: God the Father seated on the throne, and Christ as the Lamb who was slain. The Lamb is standing and has seven horns and seven eyes. The horns denote the complete strength of God (Christ), and the eyes denote Christ's all-seeing ability to search out everything.

> And he came and took the book out of the right hand of him that sat upon the throne. And when he had taken the book, the four beasts and four *and* twenty elders fell down before the Lamb, having every one of them harps, and golden vials full of odours, which are the prayers of saints.

I believe because John sees everyone around the throne holding a harp, this is why people believe that those who are in heaven strum a harp. John also sees everyone holding a bowl or censer filled with incense (the prayers of the earthly saints); see Revelation 5:8.

Next, John hears singing. Because there is no specific scripture to indicate that angels sing, I believe that the singers are humans.

> And they sung a new song, saying, Thou art worthy to take the book, and to open the seals thereof: for thou wast slain, and hast redeemed us to God by thy blood out of every kindred, and tongue, and people, and nation; And hast made us unto our God kings and priests: and we shall reign on the earth. (Rev. 5:9–10)

John hears the voice of many messengers, not singing.

> And I beheld, and I heard the voice of many angels' round about the throne and the beasts and the elders: and the number of them was ten thousand times ten thousand, and thousands of thousands; Saying with a loud voice, Worthy is the Lamb that was slain to receive power, and riches, and wisdom, and strength, and honour, and glory, and blessing.

Next, John hears what all creatures say.

> And every creature which is in heaven, and on the earth, and under the earth, and such as are in the sea, and all that are in them, heard I saying, Blessing, and honour, and glory, and power, *be* unto him that sitteth upon the throne, and unto the Lamb for ever and ever. And the four beasts said, Amen. And the four *and* twenty elders fell down and worshipped him that liveth for ever and ever.

John has told us about the scroll and its seals. Let's continue in chapter 6.

CHAPTER 6

In Revelation 6, John sees Jesus open the first of the seven seals. The first four seals loose the Four Horsemen of the Apocalypse.

> And I saw when the Lamb opened one of the seals, and I heard, as it were the noise of thunder, one of the four beasts saying, Come and see. And I saw, and behold a white horse: and he that sat on him had a bow; and a crown was given unto him: and he went forth conquering, and to conquer.

The first horseman that John sees is the one called the antichrist by the Church; the prophet Daniel called him the Man of Lawlessness—literally, the Man without God's Torah (Law). We would say that he is completely against God's law. John sees that the first rider is on a white horse. The rider is also given a crown and a bow but no arrows. Yet we are told the rider goes forth conquering and to conquer. This means the rider (the antichrist) conquers by diplomacy! He does not make war—not yet!

> And when he had opened the second seal, I heard the second beast say, Come and see. And there went out another horse *that was* red: and *power* was given to him that sat thereon to take peace from the earth, and that they should kill one another: and there was given unto him a great sword. (Rev. 6:3–4; emphasis added)

The second rider is seen on a fiery red horse (the color of war). Also, this rider is given power to take peace from the earth so that humans would slay each other. In addition, John sees that a sword is given to this rider. Because a sword is a symbol of war, this rider unleashes war such as never been seen before.

> And when he had opened the third seal, I heard the third beast say, Come and see. And I beheld, and lo a black horse; and he that sat on him had a pair of balances in his hand. And I heard a voice in the midst of the four beasts say, A measure of wheat for a penny, and three measures of barley for a penny; and *see* thou hurt not the oil and the wine. (Rev. 6:5–6; emphasis added)

The third rider that John sees is the rider of the black horse, and to him is given a set of scales or balances. This rider is told, "A measure (quart) of wheat for a day's wage, and three measures (quarts) of barley for a day's wage. And do not harm the oil and the wine." Imagine! A man will work an entire day just to buy himself a loaf of bread (a quart of wheat for a day's wage). Nothing would be left for his family! Because the rider is told not to harm the wine and the oil, the rich will not be affected as much.

> And when he had opened the fourth seal, I heard the voice of the fourth beast say, Come and see. And I looked, and behold a pale horse: and his name that sat on him was Death, and Hell followed with him. And power was given unto them over the fourth part of the earth, to kill with sword, and with hunger, and with death, and with the beasts of the earth. (Rev. 6:7–8)

This rider is on a pale horse (the color is actually a sickly green). To this rider, authority is given to kill up to one-fourth of the world's population! This rider can kill with the sword, with hunger, and with death, even with the wild beasts of the earth!

> And when he had opened the fifth seal, I saw under the altar the souls of them that were slain for the word of God, and for the testimony which they held: And they

cried with a loud voice, saying, How long, O Lord, holy
and true, dost thou not judge and avenge our blood on
them that dwell on the earth? (Rev. 6:9–10)

These cannot be Church Age believers. Notice they pray for vengeance
upon those who persecuted them. By praying, they are demonstrating
they are fully conscious. Our spirits live forever, either in heaven after
our earthly bodies expire or in hell and the lake of fire for unbelievers.
Church Age believers are always told to pray for all who persecute us,
not to pray for God to avenge us. Reference Stephen's prayer:

And he kneeled down, and cried with a loud voice, Lord,
lay not this sin to their charge. And when he had said
this, he fell asleep. (Acts 7:60)

And white robes were given unto every one of them;
and it was said unto them, that they should rest yet for
a little season, until their fellowservants also and their
brethren, that should be killed as they *were*, should be
fulfilled. (Rev. 6:11)

Here, the saints who are under the altar are told to wait a little longer for
all of those who would be killed would join them. They pray directly to
God the Father, and He responds directly, acknowledging they are aware
of their surroundings and what happened to them in the past.

And I beheld when he had opened the sixth seal, and, lo,
there was a great earthquake; and the sun became black
as sackcloth of hair, and the moon became as blood.
(Rev. 6:12)

This verse has caused much debate. The idea that the stars fell from
heaven has been interpreted as the results of a nuclear explosion. Others
believe the verse references volcanic explosions that spew ash into the
atmosphere. I tend to believe the latter is the more likely scenario. Given
the previous verse, an earthquake of supernatural origin has occurred.
An earthquake (of which there are five mentioned in the Book of
Revelation) that could cause destruction of this level would have to

originate with God. During the first seal judgments, the antichrist was the cause of these judgments. Even though God released the judgments in their own time, this is the first judgment that God releases upon the unrepentant earth! The fact that the sun became black as a sackcloth of hair and the moon became as blood indicates that something happened in the earth's atmosphere. As recently as May 19, 1980, Mount Saint Helens erupted and caused the sun to blacken, and the moon took on a reddish appearance at nighttime. The earthquake mentioned here obviously triggers a volcanic explosion that has never been seen before on earth! Krakatoa's eruption in 1883 would be a firecracker compared to this. The earthquake here is of a level that shows God's displeasure with the world.

> And the stars of heaven fell unto the earth, even as a fig tree casteth her untimely figs, when she is shaken of a mighty wind. (Rev. 6:13)

The stars here are most likely a severe meteor shower. It could also have a double reference to demons being confined to the earth itself.

> And the heaven departed as a scroll when it is rolled together; and every mountain and island were moved out of their places. (Rev. 6:14)

Scholars believe this is a reference to the atmospheric heaven and the description of heaven being departed like a scroll being rolled up; every mountain and island moved out of its place is a nuclear holocaust. The exact number of weapons used is something that cannot be determined from the text of the Bible.

> And the kings of the earth, and the great men, and the rich men, and the chief captains, and the mighty men, and every bondman, and every free man, hid themselves in the dens and in the rocks of the mountains. (Rev. 6:15)

Here, rich and poor, free and enslaved, try to hide in caves, bomb shelters, and basements from God the Father, not realizing that His Spirit is everywhere (omnipresent) and knows where every man, woman, and child is.

> And said to the mountains and rocks, Fall on us, and hide us from the face of him that sitteth on the throne, and from the wrath of the Lamb: For the great day of his wrath is come; and who shall be able to stand? (Rev. 6:16–17)

Here, those same people pray to their false gods (Mother Nature) in hopes of being saved from the wrath of God and the wrath of the Lamb of God. It is sad that humanity acknowledges Him now but still refuses to repent. Imagine a worldwide prayer event but not to Jesus Christ Himself! And to think A&E Network censored Phil Robertson of *Duck Dynasty* for condemning the very sins that Christ Himself will punish during the tribulation period.

CHAPTER 7

Separation of 144,000 Jewish Believers

Beginning with this chapter, not only does the tribulation continue, but four messengers (angels) are told to stop the four winds from blowing upon the earth, the sea, or any tree—but only after the servants of the Most High God are sealed with a mark on their foreheads.

> And after these things I saw four angels standing on the four corners of the earth, holding the four winds of the earth, that the wind should not blow on the earth, nor on the sea, nor on any tree. And I saw another angel ascending from the east, having the seal of the living God: and he cried with a loud voice to the four angels, to whom it was given to hurt the earth and the sea. (Rev. 7:1–2)

John sees another angel coming up from the rising sun, the east, who is holding the seal of the living God (the Father, the Son, and the Holy Spirit). This angel talks to the four angels who are going to hold back the four winds.

> Saying, Hurt not the earth, neither the sea, nor the trees, till we have sealed the servants of our God in their foreheads. (Rev. 7:3)

This is the second time in the Bible that such a sealing of God's elect occurs. The first time is found in Ezekiel with a mark upon their foreheads.

And the glory of the God of Israel was gone up from the cherub, whereupon he was, to the threshold of the house. And he called to the man clothed with linen, which *had* the writer's inkhorn by his side; And the LORD said unto him, Go through the midst of the city, through the midst of Jerusalem, and set a mark upon the foreheads of the men that sigh and that cry for all the abominations that be done in the midst thereof. And to the others he said in mine hearing, Go ye after him through the city, and smite: let not your eye spare, neither have ye pity: Slay utterly old *and* young, both maids, and little children, and women: but come not near any man upon whom *is* the mark; and begin at my sanctuary. Then they began at the ancient men which *were* before the house. (Ezek. 9:3–6; emphasis added)

This mark, according to scholars, would have been a lowercase Tau, the last letter of the Hebrew alphabet, which to us looks amazingly like the cross upon which Jesus was crucified.

And I heard the number of them which were sealed: *and there were* sealed an hundred *and* forty *and* four thousand of all the tribes of the children of Israel. Of the tribe of Juda *were* sealed twelve thousand. Of the tribe of Reuben *were* sealed twelve thousand. Of the tribe of Gad *were* sealed twelve thousand. Of the tribe of Aser *were* sealed twelve thousand. Of the tribe of Nepthalim *were* sealed twelve thousand. Of the tribe of Manasses *were* sealed twelve thousand. Of the tribe of Simeon *were* sealed twelve thousand. Of the tribe of Levi *were* sealed twelve thousand. Of the tribe of Issachar *were* sealed twelve thousand. Of the tribe of Zabulon *were* sealed twelve thousand. Of the tribe of Joseph *were* sealed twelve thousand. Of the tribe of Benjamin *were* sealed twelve thousand. (Rev. 7:4–8; emphasis added)

At this point, I need to point out that the half-tribe of Manasseh is mentioned but not the half-tribe of Ephraim. The latter half-tribe is replaced by his father, Joseph. Normally, the tribe of Joseph is broken in two with the half-tribes of Manasseh and Ephraim. Due to the unfaithfulness of the latter, the half-tribe of Ephraim is replaced with Joseph. See Jacob's original blessing, beginning in Genesis.

> And Joseph brought them out from between his knees, and he bowed himself with his face to the earth. And Joseph took them both, Ephraim in his right hand toward Israel's left hand, and Manasseh in his left hand toward Israel's right hand, and brought *them* near unto him. And Israel stretched out his right hand, and laid *it* upon Ephraim's head, who *was* the younger, and his left hand upon Manasseh's head, guiding his hands wittingly; for Manasseh *was* the firstborn. And he blessed Joseph, and said, God, before whom my fathers Abraham and Isaac did walk, the God which fed me all my life long unto this day, The Angel which redeemed me from all evil, bless the lads; and let my name be named on them, and the name of my fathers Abraham and Isaac; and let them grow into a multitude in the midst of the earth. And when Joseph saw that his father laid his right hand upon the head of Ephraim, it displeased him: and he held up his father's hand, to remove it from Ephraim's head unto Manasseh's head. And Joseph said unto his father, Not so, my father: for this *is* the firstborn; put thy right hand upon his head. And his father refused, and said, I know *it*, my son, I know *it*: he also shall become a people, and he also shall be great: but truly his younger brother shall be greater than he, and his seed shall become a multitude of nations. And he blessed them that day, saying, In thee shall Israel bless, saying, God make thee as Ephraim and as Manasseh: and he set Ephraim before Manasseh. And Israel said unto Joseph, Behold, I die: but God shall be with you, and bring you again unto the land of your fathers. Moreover I have given to thee one portion above thy brethren, which I took out of the hand of the Amorite with my sword and with my bow. (Gen. 48:12–22)

See also Genesis 49:1—28:

And Jacob called unto his sons, and said, Gather yourselves together, that I may tell you *that* which shall befall you in the last days. Gather yourselves together, and hear, ye sons of Jacob; and hearken unto Israel your father. Reuben, thou *art* my firstborn, my might, and the beginning of my strength, the excellency of dignity, and the excellency of power: Unstable as water, thou shalt not excel; because thou wentest up to thy father's bed; then defiledst thou *it:* he went up to my couch. Simeon and Levi *are* brethren; instruments of cruelty *are in* their habitations. O my soul, come not thou into their secret; unto their assembly, mine honour, be not thou united: for in their anger they slew a man, and in their selfwill they digged down a wall. Cursed *be* their anger, for *it was* fierce; and their wrath, for it was cruel: I will divide them in Jacob, and scatter them in Israel. Judah, thou *art he* whom thy brethren shall praise: thy hand *shall be* in the neck of thine enemies; thy father's children shall bow down before thee. Judah *is* a lion's whelp: from the prey, my son, thou art gone up: he stooped down, he couched as a lion, and as an old lion; who shall rouse him up? The sceptre shall not depart from Judah, nor a lawgiver from between his feet, until Shiloh come; and unto him *shall* the gathering of the people *be.* Binding his foal unto the vine, and his ass's colt unto the choice vine; he washed his garments in wine, and his clothes in the blood of grapes: His eyes *shall be* red with wine, and his teeth white with milk. Zebulun shall dwell at the haven of the sea; and he *shall be* for an haven of ships; and his border *shall be* unto Zidon. Issachar *is* a strong ass couching down between two burdens: And he saw that rest *was* good, and the land that *it was* pleasant; and bowed his shoulder to bear, and became a servant unto tribute. Dan shall judge his people, as one of the tribes of Israel. Dan shall be a serpent by the way, an adder in the path, that biteth the horse heels, so that his rider shall fall backward. I have waited for thy salvation, O LORD. Gad, a troop shall overcome him: but he shall overcome at the last. Out of Asher his bread *shall be* fat, and he shall yield royal dainties. Naphtali *is* a hind let loose: he giveth goodly words. Joseph *is* a fruitful bough, *even* a fruitful bough by a well; *whose* branches run over the wall: The archers have sorely grieved him, and shot *at him,* and hated him: But his bow abode in strength, and the arms of his hands were made strong by the hands of the mighty *God* of Jacob; (from thence *is* the shepherd, the stone of Israel:) *Even* by the God of thy father, who shall help thee; and by the Almighty, who shall bless thee with blessings of heaven above, blessings of the deep that lieth under, blessings of the breasts, and of the womb: The blessings of thy father have prevailed above the blessings of my progenitors unto the utmost bound of the everlasting hills: they shall be on the head of Joseph, and on the crown of the head of him that was separate from his brethren. Benjamin shall ravin *as* a wolf: in the morning he shall devour the prey, and at night he shall divide the spoil. All these *are* the twelve tribes of Israel: and this *is it* that their father spake unto them, and blessed them; every one according to his blessing he blessed them. (emphasis added)

I know a pastor who blatantly teaches that no Gentiles will be saved during the tribulation period. Look carefully at the following verses.

> After this I looked and saw a great crowd which no one was able to count, out of all nations and tribes and peoples and tongues, standing before the throne and before the Lamb, dressed in white robes, and palm branches in their hands, and crying out with a loud voice, saying, "Deliverance belongs to our Elohim who sits on the throne, and to the Lamb!" (Rev. 7:9–10)

The previous verses specifically state all nations (ethnic backgrounds) and tribes (lineages) and peoples (races) and tongues (languages) are standing before the throne of God.

And all the angels stood round about the throne, and *about* the elders and the four beasts, and fell before the throne on their faces, and worshipped God, Saying, Amen: Blessing, and glory, and wisdom, and thanksgiving, and honour, and power, and might, *be* unto our God for ever and ever. Amen. And one of the elders answered, saying unto me, What are these which are arrayed in white robes? and whence came they? (Rev. 7:11–13)

Notice the question one of the elders poses to John, and his response.

And I said unto him, Sir, thou knowest. And he said to me, These are they which came out of great tribulation, and have washed their robes, and made them white in the blood of the Lamb. (Rev. 7:14)

John did not recognize these believers even though their words clearly told him that they were numbered among the redeemed of the Lord.

Therefore are they before the throne of God, and serve him day and night in his temple: and he that sitteth on the throne shall dwell among them. They shall hunger no more, neither thirst any more; neither shall the sun light on them, nor any heat. For the Lamb which is in the midst of the throne shall feed them, and shall lead them unto living fountains of waters: and God shall wipe away all tears from their eyes. (Rev. 7:15–17)

Because they came out of the tribulation, God the Father promises them eternal rest and a special place of honor before Him and the Lamb they faithfully served on earth.

CHAPTER 8

The Judgments Intensify

Revelation 8 begins with the seventh seal being opened and the seven trumpet judgments being unleashed upon the earth. Even more perplexing is the strange silence in heaven for a space of half an hour.

> And when he had opened the seventh seal, there was silence in heaven about the space of half an hour. (Rev 8:1)

Here, there are two events occurring. The first is the seventh seal is opened. Second, there is silence in heaven. Compare this to the last half of Revelation 4:8, "and they rest not day and night, saying, Holy, holy, holy, Lord God Almighty, which was, and is, and is to come."

Because the four living creatures never stop saying, "Holy, holy, holy, Lord God Almighty," something happened in heaven that no angel or human has ever seen. In Psalm 68:1, King David says, "Let God arise, let his enemies be scattered," and in Psalm 76:9, King David again says, "When God arose to judgment, to save all the meek of the earth. Selah."

In the Old Testament times, when judgment was set, the judge or king stood up to signify that judgment would commence. We know from scripture that God's Holy Spirit goes to and fro throughout the earth.

> For the eyes of the LORD run to and fro throughout the whole earth, to shew himself strong in the behalf of them whose heart is perfect toward him. Herein thou hast done foolishly: therefore from henceforth thou shalt have wars. (2 Chron. 16:9.)

This allows God to see and hear everything that happens. We know that Jesus stood up to receive the spirit of Stephen when he was stoned to death. Nowhere in the scripture do we ever see God the Father standing up, although believers have longed for this day to occur. To finally see God the Father stand and show that judgment is set and will now occur causes all in heaven to suddenly remain silent for a span of half an hour. Imagine it: we will see something that has never been seen since the beginning of creation.

> And I saw the seven angels which stood before God; and to them were given seven trumpets. (Rev. 8:2)

Next, John sees seven angels standing before the Lord, and to these seven angels are given seven trumpets. And with these seven trumpets come seven extreme judgments.

> And another angel came and stood at the altar, having a golden censer; and there was given unto him much incense, that he should offer *it* with the prayers of all saints upon the golden altar which was before the throne. (Rev. 8:2; emphasis added)

Now John sees another angel approach the altar, and this angel receives a golden censer (bowl) filled with much incense. The angel is to offer the incense, which is the prayers of all saints upon the golden altar before the throne.

> And the smoke of the incense, *which came* with the prayers of the saints, ascended up before God out of the angel's hand. (Rev. 8:2; emphasis added)

Now the angel has offered the prayers of the saints, which ascend up before God out of the angel's hand.

> And the angel took the censer, and filled it with fire of the altar, and cast *it* into the earth: and there were voices, and thunderings, and lightnings, and an earthquake. (Rev. 8:2) [italics used by original publisher of the translation I quoted.] emphasis added)

This same angel now takes the censer and fills it with fire of the altar. Then the same fire is cast down upon the earth itself. John hears voices and thunderings, and he sees lightning and an earthquake. All are symbolic of judgments that have been decreed upon the earth.

> And the seven angels which had the seven trumpets prepared themselves to sound. The first angel sounded, and there followed hail and fire mingled with blood, and they were cast upon the earth: and the third part of trees was burnt up, and all green grass was burnt up. (Rev. 8:6–7)

At the first trumpet, hail and fire and blood strike the vegetation. one-third of all trees on the earth die, as well as all of the green grass.

> And the second angel sounded, and as it were a great mountain burning with fire was cast into the sea: and the third part of the sea became blood. (Rev. 8:8)

At the second trumpet, a fiery mountainlike star falls on the earth, causing one-third of the seas to become blood. I believe this is a great asteroid or comet that strikes the earth. Note that even one-third of all ships are destroyed by this "star."

> And the third part of the creatures which were in the sea, and had life, died; and the third part of the ships were destroyed. And the third angel sounded, and there fell a great star from heaven, burning as it were a lamp, and it fell upon the third part of the rivers, and upon the fountains of waters. (Rev. 8:9–10)

The third trumpet affects the seas, the rivers, and the springs of water. Like the "star" from the second trumpet, this is described as a great star fallen from heaven. This star is even given a name, Wormwood (which means "bitterness"). This name in the Ukrainian language is translated as Chernobyl, leading me to believe that the "star" is highly radioactive. It makes one-third of all the water on earth, undrinkable.

And the name of the star is called Wormwood: and the third part of the waters became wormwood; and many men died of the waters, because they were made bitter. And the fourth angel sounded, and the third part of the sun was smitten, and the third part of the moon, and the third part of the stars; so as the third part of them was darkened, and the day shone not for a third part of it, and the night likewise. (Rev. 8:11–12)

The fourth trumpet darkens one-third of the sunlight and one-third of the moonlight. This makes the days even colder with less sunlight, and the nights are even more depressing.

And I beheld, and heard an angel flying through the midst of heaven, saying with a loud voice, Woe, woe, woe, to the inhabiters of the earth by reason of the other voices of the trumpet of the three angels, which are yet to sound! (Rev. 8:13)

Now John hears an angel flying through the midst of heaven itself, proclaiming in a loud voice, "Woe, woe, woe, to the inhabiters of the earth by reason of the other voices of the trumpet of the three angels, which are yet to sound!"

As though the previous four trumpets were not bad enough, the last three trumpets release judgments that are even more terrifying!

CHAPTER 9

The Judgments Get Worse

And the fifth angel sounded, and I saw a star fall from heaven unto the earth: and to him was given the key of the bottomless pit. (Rev. 9:1)

Here, John hears the fifth angel sound his trumpet. In addition, John sees a star fall from heaven to the earth. I believe this is Satan falling from heaven to the earth. In addition, the star John sees is given the key of the bottomless pit.

Compare this to 2 Peter 2:4.

For if God spared not the angels that sinned, but cast *them* down to hell, and delivered *them* into chains of darkness, to be reserved unto judgment. (Rev. 9:1; emphasis added)

I believe the bottomless pit is the Bible's name for what we call a black hole. Astronomers' description of what a black hole would be like lends credibility to this theory. Astronomers believe that a black hole has such strong gravity that nothing, not even light, can escape. Another way to look at this is to say that the black hole has chains of everlasting darkness because nothing can escape on its own. It would no doubt feel like one is in a prison of everlasting darkness.

And he opened the bottomless pit; and there arose a smoke out of the pit, as the smoke of a great furnace;

and the sun and the air were darkened by reason of the
smoke of the pit. (Rev. 9:2)

Here, the fallen angel opens the bottomless pit, and smoke arises out
of the pit, like that of a great furnace. [While scientists believe that
nothing can escape a Black Hole. I believe the smoke here is caused by
the opening of the bottomless pit with the key, the fallen angel was given]
This causes the sun and air to be darkened by reason of the smoke of the
pit. Also the smoke may be symbolic of the demon horde released by the
fallen angel with the key.

And there came out of the smoke locusts upon the earth:
and unto them was given power, as the scorpions of the
earth have power. (Rev. 9:3)

Next, John sees coming out of the smoke a swarm of locusts, and unto
these locusts was given power, as the scorpions of the earth have power.
I believe these locusts are demons who fell with Lucifer; see Isaiah 14:12–
17 and Ezekiel 28:11–15.

How art thou fallen from heaven, O Lucifer, son of the
morning! *how* art thou cut down to the ground, which
didst weaken the nations! For thou hast said in thine
heart, I will ascend into heaven, I will exalt my throne
above the stars of God: I will sit also upon the mount of
the congregation, in the sides of the north: I will ascend
above the heights of the clouds; I will be like the most
High. Yet thou shalt be brought down to hell, to the sides
of the pit. They that see thee shall narrowly look upon
thee, *and* consider thee, *saying, Is* this the man that made
the earth to tremble, that did shake kingdoms; *That* made
the world as a wilderness, and destroyed the cities thereof;
that opened not the house of his prisoners? (Isa. 14:12–17)

Moreover the word of the LORD came unto me, saying,
Son of man, take up a lamentation upon the king of
Tyrus, and say unto him, Thus saith the Lord GOD;
Thou sealest up the sum, full of wisdom, and perfect

in beauty. Thou hast been in Eden the garden of God; every precious stone *was* thy covering, the sardius, topaz, and the diamond, the beryl, the onyx, and the jasper, the sapphire, the emerald, and the carbuncle, and gold: the workmanship of thy tabrets and of thy pipes was prepared in thee in the day that thou wast created. Thou *art* the anointed cherub that covereth; and I have set thee *so:* thou wast upon the holy mountain of God; thou hast walked up and down in the midst of the stones of fire. Thou *wast* perfect in thy ways from the day that thou wast created, till iniquity was found in thee. (Ezek. 28:11–15)

And it was commanded them that they should not hurt the grass of the earth, neither any green thing, neither any tree; but only those men which have not the seal of God in their foreheads. (Rev. 9:4)

These locusts were commanded that they should not hurt the grass of the earth, nor any green thing, nor any tree, but only those men who have not the seal of God on their foreheads; see Revelation 7:3 and Ezekiel 9:6.

Saying, Hurt not the earth, neither the sea, nor the trees, till we have sealed the servants of our God in their foreheads. (Rev. 7:3)

Slay utterly old *and* young, both maids, and little children, and women: but come not near any man upon whom *is* the mark; and begin at my sanctuary. Then they began at the ancient men which *were* before the house. (Ezek. 9:6; emphasis added)

Normal locusts would not attack people but rather vegetation. These locusts are commanded to harm only those people who do not have the seal of God on their foreheads.

And to them it was given that they should not kill them, but that they should be tormented five months: and their torment *was* as the torment of a scorpion, when he striketh a man. (Rev. 9:5; emphasis added)

Here, those who get stung by the scorpion-demons will feel as though they have been stung by a real scorpion.

And in those days shall men seek death, and shall not find it; and shall desire to die, and death shall flee from them. (Rev. 9:6)

Further, these locusts are forbidden from killing humans, but they are allowed to torment them for five months (150 days). Note that Death will be sought by people, but Death will flee from them. Death fears no man, woman, or child. Yet Death will not be found by any unbeliever. Next, we will examine the description of these locusts.

And the shapes of the locusts *were* like unto horses prepared unto battle; and on their heads *were* as it were crowns like gold, and their faces *were* as the faces of men. And they had hair as the hair of women, and their teeth were as *the teeth* of lions.
And they had breastplates, as it were breastplates of iron; and the sound of their wings *was* as the sound of chariots of many horses running to battle.
And they had tails like unto scorpions, and there were stings in their tails: and their power *was* to hurt men five months.
And they had a king over them, *which is* the angel of the bottomless pit, whose name in the Hebrew tongue *is* Abaddon, but in the Greek tongue hath *his* name Apollyon. (Rev. 9:7–11; emphasis added)

Both names mean *Destroyer.*

Starting in verse 7, we are told that the locusts look like horses prepared for battle, and on their heads are crowns like gold. The faces of these locusts look like men (intelligence). In verse 8, we are told that these locusts also have hair of women (beauty or attractiveness), and their teeth are as the teeth of lions (ability to tear apart and devour). In verse 9, we learn that these locusts have breastplates of iron because iron was the strongest substance known then. The breastplates of iron indicate the strength and resiliency of these locust-demons.

> One woe is past; *and,* behold, there come two woes more hereafter. (Rev. 9:12; emphasis added)

Here, we learn that the fifth trumpet has sounded—the first of the last three woes.

> And the sixth angel sounded, and I heard a voice from the four horns of the golden altar which is before God. (Rev. 9:13)

The sixth angel sounds the sixth trumpet, starting the second of the last three woes. This invokes a voice to be heard from the four horns of the golden altar, which is before God. The next verse outlines what the voice says to the sixth angel.

> Saying to the sixth angel which had the trumpet, Loose the four angels which are bound in the great river Euphrates. (Rev. 9:14)

Instead of translating the words as "in the great river Euphrates," it should be translated "at the great River Euphrates." This boundary we know better as the 10/40 Window, the heart of Islam. These fallen angels or demons cannot yet cross the Euphrates River because it is part of the land God promised to Israel.

See Joshua 1:3– 4.

> Every place that the sole of your foot shall tread upon, that have I given unto you, as I said unto Moses. From the wilderness and this Lebanon *even unto the great river, the river Euphrates,* all the land of the Hittites, and unto the great sea toward the going down of the sun, shall be your coast. (emphasis added)

And the four angels were loosed, which were prepared
for an hour, and a day, and a month, and a year, for to
slay the third part of men. (Rev. 9:15)

Verse 15 tells us why the angels (demons) were loosed. They are to bring
destruction on the human race for one year, one month, one day, and
one hour! Until the end of that span of time, they are free to do whatever
they please.

And the number of the army of the horsemen *were* two
hundred thousand thousand: and I heard the number of
them. (Rev. 9:3; emphasis added)

Here, most scholars (myself included) thought this was a human army!
As I prepared this study and was praying about this verse, the Lord
prompted me to read carefully the next verse. Verse 17 does not support
this previous opinion but rather supports the idea that John heard and
saw an army of two hundred million demons. The description of the
riders is not human!

And thus I saw the horses in the vision, and them that sat
on them, having breastplates of fire, and of jacinth, and
brimstone: and the heads of the horses *were* as the heads
of lions; and out of their mouths issued fire and smoke
and brimstone. (Rev. 9:17; emphasis added)

The breastplates of fire, jacinth, and brimstone are associated with
demons and were not to be taken figuratively, as I thought when I was
younger. Now, I believe the army consists of demonic spirits that drive
a human army! If one looks at the description of the riders, breastplates
of fire, jacinth, and brimstone indicate this is a spiritual application. The
fire speaks of destruction coming upon humankind. The jacinth speaks
of a purple color, hence royalty. The brimstone is normally associated
with sulfur or demons. Now, as to the horses themselves, their heads
were as the heads of lions, and out of their mouths issued fire and smoke
and brimstone. All three speak of demonic power!

By these three was the third part of men killed, by the fire, and by the smoke, and by the brimstone, which issued out of their mouths. (Rev. 9:18)

This verse can be taken literally as gunpowder. I believe there is both a physical application and a spiritual one here. These demons lead a murder spree that encompasses one-third of humanity.

For their power is in their mouth, and in their tails: for their tails *were* like unto serpents, and had heads, and with them they do hurt. (Rev. 9:19; emphasis added)

Verse 19 tells us these riders have power in their mouth, indicating that the riders speak destruction; in addition, the riders have power in their tails.

And the rest of the men which were not killed by these plagues yet repented not of the works of their hands, that they should not worship devils, and idols of gold, and silver, and brass, and stone, and of wood: which neither can see, nor hear, nor walk. (Rev. 9:20)

Verse 20 tells us that those who survived the death and destruction still will not repent of their sins! Humans continue to worship demons and idols of gold, silver, brass, stone, and wood. People have become so hard-hearted that they have no room in their hearts for the true living God!

Neither repented they of their murders, nor of their sorceries, nor of their fornication, nor of their thefts. (Rev. 9:21)

Verse 21 goes on to the add additional sins that humans would not repent of. It is incredible that humankind was so hardened that even after all the miracles and plagues and judgments they have experienced, humanity chooses not to turn to the living Savior in repentance.

CHAPTER 10

John Sees Angels with a Message

In Revelation 10, our focus changes from humans to angels. Although humans and the earth are still the target of God's holy judgments, John is given an intermission where he sees a second angel descending from heaven. Notice that unlike the "star that had fallen" mentioned in the previous chapter, this angel descends deliberately from heaven, indicating he is sent by the Father to deliver a special message. Even the appearance of the angel is far different from any previous appearance of an angel sent by God. John describes this as a "mighty angel." In fact, who John sees here is probably one of the archangels. Some scholars believe this angel is actually Christ himself. Although in the Old Testament, appearances of the "Angel of the Lord" was actually a preincarnate appearance of Christ Himself, I am among those who believe this angel is in fact Christ Himself. Here, Christ appears in human form now, not as an angel. Let's jump ahead a few verses and notice something this angel does that convinces me that this is more than just an angel.

In verses 5 and 6, this angel stands upon the sea and upon the earth with an uplifted hand and swears by Him who lives forever and ever, who created heaven and the things therein, and the earth and the sea and the things that are therein, that there should be time no longer.

The description (Rev. 10:1) does make one believe that this could be Christ Himself. Even though Christ Himself is part of the God-head, He still submits Himself to His Father (God) because He swears by someone greater than Himself. I believe this is Christ Himself. The description will now be examined as evidence: First, the appearance of the angel is "clothed with a cloud." We are told in the Old Testament that God is clothed (surrounded) by a cloud.

Clouds and darkness *are* round about him: righteousness and judgment *are* the habitation of his throne. A fire goeth before him, and burneth up his enemies round about. (Ps. 97:2–3; emphasis added)

Next, there is a rainbow upon his head. The rainbow reminds God of His promise to Noah and humanity to never again destroy the earth with a flood. Next time, He will use fire! Next is the appearance of the angel's face was as it were the sun. Christ's face is enveloped in a cloud in Matthew 17:5.

While he yet spake, behold, a bright cloud overshadowed them: and behold a voice out of the cloud, which said, This is my beloved Son, in whom I am well pleased; hear ye him.

Saul of Tarsus (Paul) saw Jesus as bright as the sun.

And as he journeyed, he came near Damascus: and suddenly there shined round about him a light from heaven. (Acts 9:3)

Finally, the angel John sees has feet as pillars of fire. This speaks of Christ's righteous judgments!

And his feet like unto fine brass, as if they burned in a furnace; and his voice as the sound of many waters. (Rev. 1:15)

Although here the feet appear as pillars of fire, fire is used by God to purify or cleanse something or someone. Although Christ is the second member of the Godhead and cocreator of the universe, His Father is the one who sets everything in motion. Hence the fact that this angel is probably Christ Himself! The fact that the angel stands upon the earth and sea leads me to believe that the angel is really Christ Himself, preparing to take possession of the earth!

And I saw another mighty angel come down from heaven, clothed with a cloud: and a rainbow *was* upon his head, and his face *was* as it were the sun, and his feet as pillars of fire: And he had in his hand a little book open: and he set his right foot upon the sea, and *his* left *foot* on the earth, And cried with a loud voice, as *when* a lion roareth: and when he had cried, seven thunders uttered their voices. And when the seven thunders had uttered their voices, I was about to write: and I heard a voice from heaven saying unto me, Seal up those things which the seven thunders uttered, and write them not. (Rev. 10:1–4)

John starts to record what he heard the seven thunders say. He is told not to write down what he heard but to seal it up and not reveal what he heard. The seven thunders are seven unnamed judgments that God has pronounced upon the earth. The seals, trumpets, and bowls tell us of twenty-one definite judgments, yet here are seven surprise judgments God has in store for an unbelieving world!

And the angel which I saw stand upon the sea and upon the earth lifted up his hand to heaven, And sware by him that liveth for ever and ever, who created heaven, and the things that therein are, and the earth, and the things that therein are, and the sea, and the things which are therein, that there should be time no longer. (Rev. 10:5–6)

Revelation 10 would be best described as a parenthesis between the sixth and seventh trumpet blasts. This break is similar to the break in chapter 7 (between the sixth and seventh seal judgments).

But in the days of the voice of the seventh angel, when he shall begin to sound, the mystery of God should be finished, as he hath declared to his servants the prophets. (Rev. 10:7)

In verse 7, we are told that the mystery of God is finished, and judgment is set upon the earth.

> And the voice which I heard from heaven spake unto me again, and said, Go *and* take the little book which is open in the hand of the angel which standeth upon the sea and upon the earth. (Rev. 10:8; emphasis added)

In this verse, John is told to go take the little book (scroll) from the angel (Christ) who stands upon the sea and the earth. John does this and in the next verse is given instructions.

> And I went unto the angel, and said unto him, Give me the little book. And he said unto me, Take *it,* and eat it up; and it shall make thy belly bitter, but it shall be in thy mouth sweet as honey. (Rev. 10:9; emphasis added)

John is warned that although the scroll will taste sweet in his mouth, once it gets to his belly, it will be bitter. The sweetness is in reference to those who receive His Word and accept Him as Lord and Savior. The bitterness in the belly is how unbelievers receive His Word: they want to vomit it back and reject what He says.

> And I took the little book out of the angel's hand, and ate it up; and it was in my mouth sweet as honey: and as soon as I had eaten it, my belly was bitter. And he said unto me, Thou must prophesy again before many peoples, and nations, and tongues, and kings. (Rev. 10:10–11)

In verse 11, John is told that he must prophecy before many peoples, nations, tongues, and kings. Here, he is advised that what he has seen and heard is not yet to be fulfilled.

CHAPTER 11

Two Super Witnesses

In Revelation 11, we are introduced to two super witnesses who testify of Christ for 1,260 days, divinely protected by God until the days of their witness should be completed. This is not the first reference to these men. I believe the prophet Zechariah was given a glimpse of these two men.

> Then answered I, and said unto him, What *are* these two olive trees upon the right *side* of the candlestick and upon the left *side* thereof? And I answered again, and said unto him, What *be these* two olive branches which through the two golden pipes empty the golden *oil* out of themselves? And he answered me and said, Knowest thou not what these *be?* And I said, No, my lord. Then said he, These *are* the two anointed ones, that stand by the Lord of the whole earth. (Zech. 4:11–14)

Although Zechariah has just seen a vision concerning Zerubbabel, the governor, and Joshua the high priest, I believe the vision he now sees is concerning the first reference to the two witnesses mentioned in Revelation 11:4.

> These are the two olive trees, and the two candlesticks standing before the God of the earth.

Although a form of candlesticks were used by the ancient Egyptians as early as 300 BC, the Jews were forbidden by God to use anything other than lamps filled with olive oil. Therefore what Zechariah and John see would be better translated as "lamp stands" rather than "candlesticks." Lamp stands receive oil or anointing and illuminates, whereas a candlestick only illuminates.

Revelation 11 deals with Israel's spiritual condition. By now, the Temple has been rebuilt, so the Jews have a place to gather and worship God (Elohim) according to the Mosaic law. In verse 1, John is given a reed like unto a rod (about eleven feet in length, according to *Halley's Bible Handbook*). See Ezekiel 40:5.

> And behold a wall on the outside of the house round about, and in the man's hand a measuring reed of six cubits *long* by the cubit and an hand breadth: so he measured the breadth of the building, one reed; and the height, one reed.

Because we are not told the rod is of a different length, we will conclude that the rod John is given is similar length to the one used in Ezekiel.

> And there was given me a reed like unto a rod: and the angel stood, saying, Rise, and measure the temple of God, and the altar, and them that worship therein. (Rev. 11:1)

In verse 2, John is told not to measure the Outer Court (the Court of the Gentiles). This will be trampled on by unbelievers.

Here, the timeframe wordage changes from 1,260 days to 42 months. Comparing the length of time mentioned, we find that 42 months of 30 days each according to the Hebrew calendar comes out to 1,260 days! The difference, the first reference, of 1,260 days pertains to the Jews and all tribulation believers. The 42 months are in reference to the Gentiles (world) only.

> But the court which is without the temple leave out, and measure it not; for it is given unto the Gentiles: and the holy city shall they tread under foot forty *and* two months. And I will give *power* unto my two witnesses, and they shall prophesy a thousand two hundred *and* threescore days, clothed in sackcloth. (Rev. 11:2–3; emphasis added)

I believe these two witnesses are raptured witnesses because we are told in Hebrews 9:27,

> And as it is appointed unto men once to die, but after this the judgment.

See also Genesis 3:19.

> In the sweat of thy face shalt thou eat bread, till thou return unto the ground; for out of it wast thou taken: for dust thou *art,* and unto dust shalt thou return. (emphasis added)

Also see 2 Corinthians 5:10.

> For we must all appear before the judgment seat of Christ; that every one may receive the things *done* in *his* body, according to that he hath done, whether *it be* good or bad. (emphasis added)

Although many people believe that the two witnesses are Moses and Elijah, I do not accept this. Moses died. Therefore it would fly in the face of scripture for him to return. Now, if one of the witnesses is a type of Moses (or lawgiver), and the other is a type of Elijah (or law keeper and), they are raptured.

Then the two can return to earth, witness of Christ as Lord and Savior, die because of their testimony, and be resurrected, all in accordance with the Scripture!

If the two are indeed raptured witnesses, they would easily understand the New Testament. All that would be required is for them to learn from God what He wants them to say. Hence, they would "stand before the Lord of all the earth."

Christ could easily judge these two before they return to earth or wait until they have completed their testimony and judge them just before He returns.

> And the seventh angel sounded; and there were great voices in heaven, saying, The kingdoms of this world

are become *the kingdoms* of our Lord, and of his Christ;
and he shall reign for ever and ever. (Rev. 11:15; emphasis
added)

And, behold, I come quickly; and my reward *is* with me,
to give every man according as his work shall be. (Rev.
22:12; emphasis added)

These are the two olive trees, and the two candlesticks
standing before the God of the earth. (Rev. 11:4)

We are told in the following verses that these two have incredible powers!
Not only are they protected from being killed until the 1,260 days are
completed, but they have power to send forth fire from their mouths.
This is most likely lightning!

And if any man will hurt them, fire proceedeth out of
their mouth, and devoureth their enemies: and if any
man will hurt them, he must in this manner be killed.
(Rev. 11:5)

Notice that these two are not told to pray for their enemies. Rather, they
are to destroy their enemies! If these two were witnesses who come out
of the tribulation, then they are violating Christ's command to pray for
our enemies.

These have power to shut heaven, that it rain not in
the days of their prophecy: and have power over waters
to turn them to blood, and to smite the earth with all
plagues, as often as they will. (Rev. 11:6)

These two are given power to prevent rain from falling anywhere on
the earth, and they can call down plagues as often as they want! I don't
believe mere mortals could handle that kind of power and responsibility.
Only two raptured, New Testament believers purged of all of their fallen
nature could handle this and still obey God!

And when they shall have finished their testimony, the beast that ascendeth out of the bottomless pit shall make war against them, and shall overcome them, and kill them. (Rev. 11:7)

Here, we learn that at the end of the 1,260 days, the beast that ascends out of the bottomless pit is now allowed to make war against the two witnesses and kill them, but only after their appointed time of ministry has run its course.

And their dead bodies *shall lie* in the street of the great city, which spiritually is called Sodom and Egypt, where also our Lord was crucified. (Rev. 11:8; emphasis added)

Now, even though the city where the two witnesses are killed is spiritually called Sodom and Egypt, the fact that it is also called the great city. That means the city is Jerusalem. It is spiritually called Sodom for the depravity, and it is called Egypt due to prevalence of all other sins. Finally, we are told "where our Lord was crucified."
Jesus was crucified just outside Jerusalem.

And they of the people and kindreds and tongues and nations shall see their dead bodies three days and an half, and shall not suffer their dead bodies to be put in graves. (Rev. 11:9)

These two witnesses will have so angered the world that their bodies will not be buried but left where they lie for three and a half days. There will be so much rejoicing that people will send each other gifts. Further, with the advent of satellite television, the whole world will be able to see their dead bodies at the same time.

And they that dwell upon the earth shall rejoice over them, and make merry, and shall send gifts one to another; because these two prophets tormented them that dwelt on the earth. (Rev. 11:10)

Now for the real shocker. The Holy Spirit will enter their bodies, and they will stand up, alive, in front of a world full of witnesses. Imagine the fear that will fall upon the whole world when this happens.

> And after three days and an half the Spirit of life from God entered into them, and they stood upon their feet; and great fear fell upon them which saw them. (Rev. 11:11)

Verse 12 tells us that the world (their enemies) will watch as the two witnesses ascend up to heaven in a cloud.

> And they heard a great voice from heaven saying unto them, Come up hither. And they ascended up to heaven in a cloud; and their enemies beheld them. (Rev. 11:12)

This precedes an incredible earthquake that destroys one-tenth of the city (Jerusalem). We are even told the death toll will be seven thousand and that the survivors give glory to God. They do not repent!

> And the same hour was there a great earthquake, and the tenth part of the city fell, and in the earthquake were slain of men seven thousand: and the remnant were affrighted, and gave glory to the God of heaven. (Rev. 11:13)

Now we learn that the sixth trumpet has sounded, and the seventh trumpet is going to sound quickly.

> The second woe is past; *and,* behold, the third woe cometh quickly. (Rev. 11:14)

When the seventh angel sounds the seventh trumpet, this causes great voices in heaven to speak

> And the seventh angel sounded; and there were great voices in heaven, saying, The kingdoms of this world are become *the kingdoms* of our Lord, and of his Christ;

and he shall reign for ever and ever. (Rev. 11:15; emphasis added)

The twenty-four elders who are now seated fall upon the faces and worship God, knowing that Christ is about to set up His kingdom on the earth.

And the four and twenty elders, which sat before God on their seats, fell upon their faces, and worshipped God, Saying, We give thee thanks, O Lord God Almighty, which art, and wast, and art to come; because thou hast taken to thee thy great power, and hast reigned. And the nations were angry, and thy wrath is come, and the time of the dead, that they should be judged, and that thou shouldest give reward unto thy servants the prophets, and to the saints, and them that fear thy name, small and great; and shouldest destroy them which destroy the earth. And the temple of God was opened in heaven, and there was seen in his temple the ark of his testament: and there were lightnings, and voices, and thunderings, and an earthquake, and great hail. (Rev. 11:16–19)

John sees the heavenly temple of God open, and there John sees the Ark of the Covenant. He sees lightning and hears voices and thunders, and he sees an earthquake and even great hail!

Hell on earth is about to commence!

CHAPTER 12

The Woman and Her Child

This is going to feel like we are going back to the middle of the tribulation. Well, because everything happens in the last half of the tribulation, this is what we must do to maintain the clarity of the events. The prophet Jeremiah spoke of this time.

> Alas! for that day *is* great, so that none *is* like it: it *is* even the time of Jacob's trouble; but he shall be saved out of it. (Jer. 30:7)

The apostle Paul confirms that Jacob here is Israel itself.

> And so all Israel shall be saved: as it is written, There shall come out of Sion the Deliverer, and shall turn away ungodliness from Jacob. (Rom. 11:26)

Revelation 12 looks mainly at the persecution that the nation of Israel suffers, particularly during this greatest outpouring of anti-Semitism the world has ever seen. Thankfully, the greatest outpouring of God's love for the nation of Israel and the world occurs during this time.

> And there appeared a great wonder in heaven; a woman clothed with the sun, and the moon under her feet, and upon her head a crown of twelve stars. (Rev. 12:1)

The woman here is not a human woman, as Mary Baker Eddy Glover Patterson tried to claim when she announced that she was that woman mentioned here. The founder of the Christian Science Movement seriously misquoted scripture and tried to make it fit her. The woman's offspring here is the nation of Israel, not a Gentile denomination. The woman here was originally foretold of by Joseph in a dream he shared with his brothers and then to his father, Jacob.

> And he dreamed yet another dream, and told it his brethren, and said, Behold, I have dreamed a dream more; and, behold, the sun and the moon and the eleven stars made obeisance to me. And he told *it* to his father, and to his brethren: and his father rebuked him, and said unto him, What *is* this dream that thou hast dreamed? Shall I and thy mother and thy brethren indeed come to bow down ourselves to thee to the earth? And his brethren envied him; but his father observed the saying. (Gen. 37:9–11)

> And she being with child cried, travailing in birth, and pained to be delivered. And there appeared another wonder in heaven; and behold a great red dragon, having seven heads and ten horns, and seven crowns upon his heads. (Rev. 12:2–3)

In the previous two verses, we see a woman in the pains of childbirth, and then we also see another wonder, a great red dragon (Satan) having seven heads, ten horns, and ten crowns upon his heads. The seven heads symbolize the completeness of the wisdom of the great dragon (Satan). Remember that in Ezekiel 28:12, we are told that when God created Lucifer, He created him full of wisdom.

> Son of man, take up a lamentation upon the king of Tyrus, and say unto him, Thus saith the Lord GOD; Thou sealest up the sum, full of wisdom, and perfect in beauty.

The ten horns and ten crowns are symbolic of the total control that Satan will have. Compare this to the ten toes of the great statue, seen by the prophet Daniel.

> And whereas thou sawest the feet and toes, part of potters' clay, and part of iron, the kingdom shall be divided; but there shall be in it of the strength of the iron, forasmuch as thou sawest the iron mixed with miry clay. And *as* the toes of the feet *were* part of iron, and part of clay, *so* the kingdom shall be partly strong, and partly broken. And whereas thou sawest iron mixed with miry clay, they shall mingle themselves with the seed of men: but they shall not cleave one to another, even as iron is not mixed with clay. And in the days of these kings shall the God of heaven set up a kingdom, which shall never be destroyed: and the kingdom shall not be left to other people, *but* it shall break in pieces and consume all these kingdoms, and it shall stand for ever. (Dan. 2:41–44; emphasis added)

It would appear that some nations or governments have more than one leader who ultimately reports to the great dragon (Satan). Next, we read further evidence that this is Satan himself. We are told in Revelation 12:4 that "his tail drew the third part of the stars of heaven and did cast them to the earth." This would not make sense literally, so a symbolic interpretation is in order. The third part of the stars of heaven would be the demons who were loose to travel about the second heaven (outer space). These stars or demons are now confined to the earth itself.

> And his tail drew the third part of the stars of heaven, and did cast them to the earth: and the dragon stood before the woman which was ready to be delivered, for to devour her child as soon as it was born. And she brought forth a man child, who was to rule all nations with a rod of iron: and her child was caught up unto God, and *to* his throne. (Rev. 12:4–5)

As I said earlier, the woman here is the nation of Israel. The child she gives birth to is none other than Christ Jesus Himself! Revelation 12:5 tells us that the child she gives birth to is male, and He was caught up to God and to His throne. This part of the prophecy is dealing with the first time Christ leaves earth.

The next verse jumps ahead and speaks of the time when believing Israel (those who come to accept Jesus Christ as their Lord and Savior) flee into the desert (probably the desert city of Petra), where God will supernaturally provide for these believers.

> And the woman fled into the wilderness, where she hath a place prepared of God, that they should feed her there a thousand two hundred *and* threescore days. (Rev. 12:6)

That is the total number of days that will comprise the Great Tribulation.

Next, we read about a war in heaven. Many scholars believe this war began at the time of the rapture and culminates here. Remember that chapters 12–19 run concurrently with chapters 6–11. Because a war encompasses more than one skirmish, this seems a logical conclusion. Clearly Satan and his angels (demons) do not win but are cast down to the earth itself.

> And there was war in heaven: Michael and his angels fought against the dragon; and the dragon fought and his angels, And prevailed not; neither was their place found any more in heaven. And the great dragon was cast out, that old serpent, called the Devil, and Satan, which receiveth the whole world: he was cast out into the earth, and his angels were cast out with him. (Rev. 12:7–9)

Next, we read of praise and an ominous warning for those dwelling on the earth.

> And I heard a loud voice saying in heaven, Now is come salvation, and strength, and the kingdom of our God, and the power of his Christ: for the accuser of our brethren is cast down, which accused them before our God day and night. And they overcame him by the blood of the Lamb, and by the word of their testimony; and they loved not their lives unto the death. Therefore rejoice, *ye* heavens, and ye that dwell in them. Woe to the inhabiters of the earth and of the sea! for the devil is come down unto you,

having great wrath, because he knoweth that he hath but a short time. (Rev. 12:10–12)

Notice in verse 12 that John hears a warning for the inhabitants of the earth because Satan now knows exactly how long he has left before Christ returns to set up His millennial kingdom.

And when the dragon saw that he was cast unto the earth, he persecuted the woman which brought forth the man *child*. (Rev. 12:13; emphasis added)

Sadly, Satan takes out his anger on the woman or nation of Israel.

And to the woman were given two wings of a great eagle, that she might fly into the wilderness, into her place, where she is nourished for a time, and times, and half a time, from the face of the serpent. (Rev. 12:14)

Here, God enables Jewish believers to flee into the wilderness to a hiding place to be nourished for a time (a year), times (two years), and half a time (six months). A total of three and a half years, or 42 months, or 1,260 days.

And the serpent cast out of his mouth water as a flood after the woman, that he might cause her to be carried away of the flood. (Rev. 12:15)

The serpent sends forth water as a flood after the woman. This is symbolically interpreted as water. Most likely this is the worldwide anti-Semitic attitude against Israel, which the enemy intends to use to destroy the woman. But God causes the earth to open and swallow the flood, protecting the woman as she flees.

See God's promise to Israel.

So shall they fear the name of the LORD from the west, and his glory from the rising of the sun. When the enemy shall come in like a flood, the Spirit of the LORD shall lift up a standard against him. (Isa. 59:19)

And the earth helped the woman, and the earth opened
her mouth, and swallowed up the flood which the dragon
cast out of his mouth. (Rev. 12:16)

Now the dragon is really mad at the woman and sets out to make war
with the remnant of her seed (those Jews who proclaim Jesus is Lord and
Messiah and both keep the commandments of the Mosaic Law and have
the testimony of Jesus Christ).

And the dragon was wroth with the woman, and went
to make war with the remnant of her seed, which keep
the commandments of God, and have the testimony of
Jesus Christ. (Rev. 12:17)

CHAPTER 13

The Beast and the False Prophet

In Revelation 13, we are introduced to the beast, or as he is more commonly referred to, the antichrist, and his right-hand man, the false prophet.

Before I begin this chapter, I would like to take some time to clarify a misnomer that I, along with many others, held on to. This is the idea that the antichrist would occupy the position of pope of the Catholic Church during the tribulation. While in careful study and prayer about this, the Lord revealed to me something that does not add up with this train of thought. Scholars accept that the antichrist will be a political leader and that the false prophet will be a religious leader. Based on everything I read in the scripture and from what the Lord has corrected me on, I no longer hold to the idea that the antichrist will be pope of the Catholic Church during the tribulation. I now hold the position that the false prophet, the religious leader, will be pope of the Catholic Church! I know this idea may seem bizarre to many. Consider the points I have already made. The beast, or antichrist, will be the political power. The religious power will be vested in the false prophet.

The false prophet first deceives with false miracles and then later forces all to worship the image of the beast.

> And I beheld another beast coming up out of the earth; and he had two horns like a lamb, and he spake as a dragon. And he exerciseth all the power of the first beast before him, and causeth the earth and them which dwell therein to worship the first beast, whose deadly wound was healed. And he doeth great wonders, so that he maketh fire come down from heaven on the earth in

the sight of men, And deceiveth them that dwell on the earth by *the means of* those miracles which he had power to do in the sight of the beast; saying to them that dwell on the earth, that they should make an image to the beast, which had the wound by a sword, and did live. (Rev. 13:11–14)

I will discuss the false prophet later in this chapter.

And I stood upon the sand of the sea, and saw a beast rise up out of the sea, having seven heads and ten horns, and upon his horns ten crowns, and upon his heads the name of blasphemy. (Rev. 13:1)

This verse would more accurately be translated as "he" (Satan), not "I" (John). Revelation 13:1 should really be the last verse of Revelation 12 because it continues with the persecution of the nation of Israel. Satan is standing upon the sand of the sea.

Symbolically, he is looking at the sea of humanity. He sees the beast rising up out of the sea, having seven heads (wisdom) and ten horns (complete authority over the earthly governments), and upon his horns are ten crowns. It is the earthly political power that submits to him. In addition, upon the beast's heads is written the name of blasphemy. This beast is under his control and, even though neither Satan nor the beast would admit it, ultimately under the control of God and Jesus Christ!

The second beast will be a religious figure or leader.

And the beast which I saw was like unto a leopard, and his feet were as *the feet* of a bear, and his mouth as the mouth of a lion: and the dragon gave him his power, and his seat, and great authority. (Rev. 13:2; emphasis added)

Here, Satan gives the first beast authority over the earth. Satan is still pulling the strings, but he lets the first beast think he is in charge.

And I saw one of his heads as it were wounded to death; and his deadly wound was healed: and all the world wondered after the beast. (Rev. 13:3)

This verse has been the subject of much debate. In 1977, when porno mogul Larry Flint was seriously wounded, a friend of mine actually made the claim that Larry Flint was the antichrist! Now, I agree that Larry Flint has a spirit of antichrist, but I disagree about him being the actual antichrist. Larry Flint does not possess the political clout necessary to be the antichrist. In the next verse, we learn that Satan actually gets widespread worship—something he has always wanted!

This is the one time that God allows Satan to resurrect someone.

> And they worshipped the dragon which gave power unto the beast: and they worshipped the beast, saying, Who *is* like unto the beast? who is able to make war with him? And there was given unto him a mouth speaking great things and blasphemies; and power was given unto him to continue forty *and* two months. (Rev. 13:4–5; emphasis added)

We are now told that the first beast was given a mouth, speaking great things and blasphemies, and power was given unto him to continue for forty-two months. This tells us that the first beast is a literal man, demon-possessed like no other in history. The demon or demons that possess the antichrist and the false prophet come straight out of the abyss—the same abyss mentioned in Revelation 17:8.

> The beast that thou sawest was, and is not; and shall ascend out of the bottomless pit, and go into perdition: and they that dwell on the earth shall wonder, whose names were not written in the book of life from the foundation of the world, when they behold the beast that was, and is not, and yet is.

John is further told something about this king. The five heads that John saw are five kings who ruled up to John's day. One rules at the time of John (the sixth), and the seventh king would come later. This last king is the antichrist himself! This is confirmed later in Revelation 17:10.

> And there are seven kings: five are fallen, and one is, and the other is not yet come; and when he cometh, he must continue a short space.

And he opened his mouth in blasphemy against God, to blaspheme his name, and his tabernacle, and them that dwell in heaven. (Rev. 13:6)

This beast utters blasphemy against God, His name, His tabernacle, and those who dwell in heaven.

And it was given unto him to make war with the saints, and to overcome them: and power was given him over all kindreds, and tongues, and nations. (Rev. 13:7)

Many believers cite the previous when they talk about persecution of believers during the tribulation. The dragon and the two beasts are given permission by God to persecute all believers upon the earth.

And all that dwell upon the earth shall worship him, whose names are not written in the book of life of the Lamb slain from the foundation of the world. (Rev. 13:8)

Verse 8 tells us who will worship the dragon and the beast: anyone who dwells upon the earth and whose names are not written in the book of life of the Lamb. These are not believers.

If any man have an ear, let him hear. He that leadeth into captivity shall go into captivity: he that killeth with the sword must be killed with the sword. Here is the patience and the faith of the saints. (Rev. 13:9–10)

Next, we are introduced to the second beast, the false prophet. John sees this beast coming up out of the earth, symbolizing that this beast like the first, is human, and is an unbeliever. Notice that this second beast has two horns like a lamb but speaks as a dragon with great power and authority. The lamb symbolizes innocence, but the two horns indicate this lamb is anything but peaceful.

As I stated earlier in this chapter, I will now address the false prophet, whom I believe will hold the office of pope of the Catholic Church during the tribulation, perhaps even just prior to this.

In my research, I found that Bible scholar Ed Hinson appears to believe that the false prophet will likely hold the office of pope of the Catholic Church.

I would like to refer the reader to a website run by the Catholic Church pertaining to a man named St. Malachy, who accurately predicted the last 112 popes up to and including Pope Benedict XVI! Malachy lived around AD 1140, and it is said that while on a visit to Rome, he made prophecy of the next 112 popes. I have included a copy of this list as found on their website.

I even found claims on a website called malachyprophecy.com that Pope Francis will become Petrus Romanus, Peter the Roman—the final pope of the Catholic Church. Read the description above of the one who Malachy says would be Pope Benedict's successor.

"In extreme persecution, the seat of the Holy Roman Church will be occupied by Peter the Roman, who will feed the sheep through many tribulations, at the term of which the city of seven hills will be destroyed, and the formidable Judge will judge his people. The End."

> Extreme persecution? Sounds to me like the tribulation period. Peter the Roman will feed the sheep through many tribulations, at the end of which the city of seven hills will be destroyed, and the formidable judge will judge his people (Christ Himself and the judgment of all those who went through the tribulation).

> And I beheld another beast coming up out of the earth; and he had two horns like a lamb, and he spake as a dragon. (Rev. 13:11)

In verse 12, we learn that the second beast exercises all of the power of the first beast. The second beast goes on to cause all that dwell upon the earth to worship the first beast, who suffered a deadly wound but lives again.

> And he exerciseth all the power of the first beast before him, and causeth the earth and them which dwell therein to worship the first beast, whose deadly wound was healed. (Rev. 13:12)

Refer back to Revelation 13:3 for the deadly wound and subsequent healing.

> And I saw one of his heads as it were wounded to death; and his deadly wound was healed: and all the world wondered after the beast.

> And he doeth great wonders, so that he maketh fire come down from heaven on the earth in the sight of men. (Rev. 13:13)

Not only does the first beast do great wonders (miracles), but he even makes fire come down from heaven; this is probably lightning.

> And deceiveth them that dwell on the earth by *the means of* those miracles which he had power to do in the sight of the beast; saying to them that dwell on the earth, that they should make an image to the beast, which had the wound by a sword, and did live. (Rev. 13:14; emphasis added)

Sadly, the world itself will believe that the miracles the first beast performs are really signs that God is with him. Yes, God is allowing the miracles to happen, but He is not approving of the beast.

> And he had power to give life unto the image of the beast, that the image of the beast should both speak, and cause that as many as would not worship the image of the beast should be killed. (Rev. 13:15)

The image has caused much debate among readers, both scholars and laypeople. I am not sure what this image will be, but it is clear from scripture that the image is able to speak. Notice the first part of verse 15 tells us that the second beast actually gives life to the image. The word for life here is *breath* or *spirit* in the Hebrew, or *zoe* (life) or *pnuema* (spirit) in Greek.

And he causeth all, both small and great, rich and poor, free and bond, to receive a mark in their right hand, or in their foreheads. (Rev. 13:16)

Many believe this mark will be a gold or platinum microchip implanted into the recipient. I do not believe this because some people are actually allergic to gold, and platinum is too expensive! With the advances in science and technology, I believe the mark uses a SKU code to be read and a biological chip that will program itself to the person or host. Because it has already been verified by science that the forehead or right hand of the human body maintains the most constant temperature, this coincides with what scripture already told us centuries ago.

And that no man might buy or sell, save he that had the mark, or the name of the beast, or the number of his name. (Rev. 13:17)

Now, the second beast makes it mandatory to be able to purchase anything! In verse 17, we are told that only if someone has the number of his name can someone purchase. Again, I believe the number is a SKU code. See an example of UPC symbol.

The bars on the left, middle, and right all read as a 6. This could well be what scripture means when it says,

Here is wisdom. Let him that hath understanding count the number of the beast: for it is the number of a man; and his number is Six hundred threescore and six. (Rev. 13:18)

CHAPTER 14

144,000 Gentile Believers

And I looked, and, lo, a Lamb stood on the mount Sion (Zion) and with him an hundred forty *and* four thousand, having his Father's name written in their foreheads. (Rev. 14:1)

This is unlike the Jewish believers in Revelation 7.

And I heard the number of them which were sealed: *and there were* sealed an hundred *and* forty *and* four thousand of all the tribes of the children of Israel. Of the tribe of Juda *were* sealed twelve thousand. Of the tribe of Reuben *were* sealed twelve thousand. Of the tribe of Gad *were* sealed twelve thousand. Of the tribe of Aser *were* sealed twelve thousand. Of the tribe of Nepthalim *were* sealed twelve thousand. Of the tribe of Manasses *were* sealed twelve thousand. Of the tribe of Simeon *were* sealed twelve thousand. Of the tribe of Levi *were* sealed twelve thousand. Of the tribe of Issachar *were* sealed twelve thousand. Of the tribe of Zabulon *were* sealed twelve thousand. Of the tribe of Joseph *were* sealed twelve thousand. Of the tribe of Benjamin *were* sealed twelve thousand. (Rev. 7:4–8)

These are Gentile believers, unlike the Jewish believers who were identified by their particular tribe, twelve thousand from each of the twelve tribes. These believers have only their Father's name written in their foreheads. This is symbolic of you having set your mind on being a believer in Jesus Christ, and therefore you belong to Jesus and ultimately to God the Father. Under the New Covenant, our mark is the presence of the Holy Spirit renewing us and marking us as belonging to Jesus. During the tribulation, believers will be marked for the Father, even though they must individually accept the sacrificial offering Jesus made on Calvary.

> And I heard a voice from heaven, as the voice of many waters, and as the voice of a great thunder: and I heard the voice of harpers harping with their harps. (Rev. 14:2)

John hears the voice of many waters. Though waters do not normally speak, John is trying to convey how loud the voice was. John even adds that the voice sounded like a great thunder, and he hears the voice of harpers harping with their harps.

> And they sung as it were a new song before the throne, and before the four beasts, and the elders: and no man could learn that song but the hundred and forty and four thousand, which were redeemed from the earth. (Rev. 14:3)

John is not saying that no one else could sing the song these believers sing. It will be a song reserved solely for them as a reward for coming out of the tribulation period.

> These are they which were not defiled with women; for they are virgins. These are they which follow the Lamb whithersoever he goeth. These were redeemed from among men, *being* the firstfruits unto God and to the Lamb. (Rev. 14:4)

Verse 5 is the subject of much debate. Many readers believe that these believers are physically and spiritually virgins. I do not hold to the first, but do believe that these believers are undefiled spiritually and morally. A man who remains physically celibate prior to becoming married and does not involve himself in anything that would spiritually or morally contaminate him would still be considered a virgin. Nowhere does the

Bible teach chastity as a requirement. Chastity is considered a spiritual virtue.

> And in their mouth was found no guile: for they are without fault before he throne of God. (Rev. 14:5)

Here, John tells us that nothing evil was found in their mouths. Indicating that these men, did not say anything that Jesus himself would not have said to His own enemies. I must admit that I would personally fall short of this.

> And I saw another angel fly in the midst of heaven, having the everlasting gospel to preach unto them that dwell on the earth, and to every nation, and kindred, and tongue, and people. (Rev. 14:6)

Now, an angel gets to do what believers have been called on since the beginning to do: spread the Gospel! Some translations say an eagle, an angel, or a messenger is a more accurate translation. Because the end of the tribulation period is so near, humanity needs to wake up before it is too late!

> Saying with a loud voice, Fear God, and give glory to him; for the hour of his judgment is come: and worship him that made heaven, and earth, and the sea, and the fountains of waters. (Rev. 14:7)

A second angel follows, proclaiming Babylon has fallen. Personally, I believe this is reference to Rome. Because Rome (Vatican City Vatican and many people would be able to anchor off shore. There is also so much sin coming out of Rome.

> And there followed another angel, saying, Babylon is fallen, is fallen, that great city, because she made all nations drink of the wine of the wrath of her fornication. (Rev. 14:8)

A third angel follows, this one pronouncing God's judgment on all who have worshipped the beast and his image and received his mark on their foreheads or their hand. Sadly, this angel's message is the longest of the three, covering verses 9–11. In verse 10, God allows sinful humanity to drink the wine of His wrath. Then we are told that these unbelievers will be tormented with fire and brimstone in the presence of the holy angels. To me, this means that the unrepentant will be visible to the holy angels and probably us. However, God will wipe our memory of who is in hell and eventually the lake of fire, so we will not be saddened by the loss of loved ones who never accepted Jesus Christ as Lord and Savior.

> And the third angel followed them, saying with a loud voice, If any man worship the beast and his image, and receive his mark in his forehead, or in his hand, The same shall drink of the wine of the wrath of God, which is poured out without mixture into the cup of his indignation; and he shall be tormented with fire and brimstone in the presence of the holy angels, and in the presence of the Lamb: And the smoke of their torment ascendeth up for ever and ever: and they have no rest day nor night, who worship the beast and his image, and whosoever receiveth the mark of his name. (Rev. 14:9–11)

Now, God wants to encourage believers (saints) who go through the tribulation and keep the commandments of God and faith in Jesus Christ.

> Here is the patience of the saints: here are they that keep the commandments of God, and the faith of Jesus. (Rev. 14:12)

John hears a voice from heaven telling him to write, "Blessed are the dead which die in the Lord from henceforth. Yea, said the Spirit, that they may rest from their labours; and their works do follow them." (Rev. 14:13)

Here, we are told that believers who die in the Lord receive a special blessing for coming in among the last of the tribulation saints. Although there will be more, these are the beginning of the final harvest. Their works that follow them are the deeds and actions they did that God approves of.

And I heard a voice from heaven saying unto me, Write, Blessed *are* the dead which die in the Lord from henceforth: Yea, saith the Spirit, that they may rest from their labours; and their works do follow them. (Rev. 14:13)

The figure John sees here is Christ Himself, and He is about to harvest the tribulation saints. Notice that John tells us this figure looks like the Son of Man (Jesus's favorite expression to use of Himself when He was first here on earth).

And I looked, and behold a white cloud, and upon the cloud one sat like unto the Son of man, having on his head a golden crown, and in his hand a sharp sickle. And another angel came out of the temple, crying with a loud voice to him that sat on the cloud, Thrust in thy sickle, and reap: for the time is come for thee to reap; for the harvest of the earth is ripe. And he that sat on the cloud thrust in his sickle on the earth; and the earth was reaped. (Rev. 14:14–16)

Now, John sees an angel coming out of the temple in heaven. Like Christ, this angel is carrying a sharp sickle.

And another angel came out of the temple which is in heaven, he also having a sharp sickle. (Rev. 14:17)

Another angel comes out of the altar. This angel has power over fire and calls to the angel who came out of the temple to thrust his sickle into the earth and gather the clusters of the vine of the earth. The unbelievers are about to be destroyed.

And another angel came out from the altar, which had power over fire; and cried with a loud cry to him that had the sharp sickle, saying, Thrust in thy sharp sickle, and gather the clusters of the vine of the earth; for her grapes are fully ripe. And the angel thrust in his sickle into the earth, and gathered the vine of the earth, and cast *it* into the great winepress of the wrath of God. (Rev. 14:18–19)

To confirm that these are unbelievers, notice where they are tossed once they have been harvested: into the great winepress of the wrath of God.

> And the winepress was trodden without the city, and blood came out of the winepress, even unto the horse bridles, by the space of a thousand and six hundred furlongs. (Rev. 14:20)

Here, the winepress we are told is outside of Jerusalem. The death toll is so great that blood flows as deep as a horse's bridle (about four to five feet deep) and for a distance of about two hundred miles! Normally blood would clot and therefore not flow, but "Radiation sickness can cause bleeding from the nose, mouth, gums, and rectum. It can cause people to bruise easily and to bleed internally as well - and even to vomit blood.

The problems occur because radiation depletes the body of platelets, the cellular fragments in the blood that are form clots to control bleeding".[1]

If the area were hit with several nuclear detonations, then blood could easily flow for two hundred miles and probably about a half mile in width! The armies are here because God has drawn them to the Valley of Megiddo.

> And he gathered them together into a place called in the Hebrew tongue Armageddon. (Rev. 16:16)

---

[1] https://www.cbsnews.com/pictures/radiation-sickness-8-terrifying-symptoms/3/

CHAPTER 15

Judgment Is Set

Here, John sees a great and marvelous sight. The final seven judgments are ready to be launched in rapid succession!

> And I saw another sign in heaven, great and marvellous, seven angels having the seven last plagues; for in them is filled up the wrath of God. (Rev. 15:1)

These saints are given harps, and they play the Song of Moses.

> Then sang Moses and the children of Israel this song unto the LORD, and spake, saying, I will sing unto the LORD, for he hath triumphed gloriously: the horse and his rider hath he thrown into the sea. The LORD *is* my strength and song, and he is become my salvation: he *is* my God, and I will prepare him an habitation; my father's God, and I will exalt him. The LORD *is* a man of war: the LORD *is* his name. Pharaoh's chariots and his host hath he cast into the sea: his chosen captains also are drowned in the Red sea. The depths have covered them: they sank into the bottom as a stone. 6 Thy right hand, O LORD, is become glorious in power: thy right hand, O LORD, hath dashed in pieces the enemy. And in the greatness of thine excellency thou hast overthrown them that rose up against thee: thou sentest forth thy wrath, *which* consumed them as stubble. And with the blast of thy nostrils the waters were gathered together,

the floods stood upright as an heap, *and* the depths were congealed in the heart of the sea. The enemy said, I will pursue, I will overtake, I will divide the spoil; my lust shall be satisfied upon them; I will draw my sword, my hand shall destroy them. Thou didst blow with thy wind, the sea covered them: they sank as lead in the mighty waters. Who *is* like unto thee, O LORD, among the gods? who *is* like thee, glorious in holiness, fearful *in* praises, doing wonders? Thou stretchedst out thy right hand, the earth swallowed them. Thou in thy mercy hast led forth the people which thou hast redeemed: thou hast guided *them* in thy strength unto thy holy habitation. The people shall hear, *and* be afraid: sorrow shall take hold on the inhabitants of Palestina. Then the dukes of Edom shall be amazed; the mighty men of Moab, trembling shall take hold upon them; all the inhabitants of Canaan shall melt away. Fear and dread shall fall upon them; by the greatness of thine arm they shall be *as* still as a stone; till thy people pass over, O LORD, till the people pass over, which thou hast purchased. Thou shalt bring them in, and plant them in the mountain of thine inheritance, *in* the place, O LORD, *which* thou hast made for thee to dwell in, *in* the Sanctuary, O Lord, *which* thy hands have established. The LORD shall reign for ever and ever. For the horse of Pharaoh went in with his chariots and with his horsemen into the sea, and the LORD brought again the waters of the sea upon them; but the children of Israel went on dry *land* in the midst of the sea. (Exod. 15:1–19)

In addition, these saints also sing the song of the Lamb and praise God for His holiness.

And I saw as it were a sea of glass mingled with fire: and them that had gotten the victory over the beast, and over his image, and over his mark, and over the number of his name, stand on the sea of glass, having the harps of God. (Rev. 15:2)

The sea of glass John sees here is symbolic of those saints who died during the tribulation period and are now at rest. They stand on a perfectly calm sea, and nothing upsets them or troubles them. Because they remained faithful to God even to the point of death, they are given a special place in heaven. The fire indicates God judgment and approval of these saints. Notice they are not harmed or tormented by the fire.

> And they sing the song of Moses the servant of God, and the song of the Lamb, saying, Great and marvellous *are* thy works, Lord God Almighty; just and true *are* thy ways, thou King of saints. Who shall not fear thee, O Lord, and glorify thy name? for *thou* only *art* holy: for all nations shall come and worship before thee; for thy judgments are made manifest. (Rev. 15:3–4)

Here, the saints praise God for who He is.

> And after that I looked, and, behold, the temple of the tabernacle of the testimony in heaven was opened. (Rev. 15:5)

John sees the temple of the Tabernacle, after which the one on earth was modeled.

> And the seven angels came out of the temple, having the seven plagues, clothed in pure and white linen, and having their breasts girded with golden girdles. (Rev. 15:6)

Even though these are clearly angels, they function in the role of priests. Note the golden sashes around their chests. Because they are created beings, they are pure and unblemished in the sight of God and therefore can execute judgment.

> And one of the four beasts gave unto the seven angels seven golden vials full of the wrath of God, who liveth for ever and ever. (Rev. 15:7)

John sees one of the four beasts (creatures) give the seven angel-priests each a bowl or golden vial filled with the full wrath of God!

> And the temple was filled with smoke from the glory of God, and from his power; and no man was able to enter into the temple, till the seven plagues of the seven angels were fulfilled. (Rev. 15:8)

Compare this to 2 Chronicles 7:2.

> And the priests could not enter into the house of the LORD, because the glory of the LORD had filled the LORD'S house.

To confirm that He is directing everything, the glory of God fills the heavenly temple so much so that no one can enter the temple for any reason.

CHAPTER 16

The Wrath of God Is Poured Out

The bowls or vials are emptied in rapid succession. Once the command to empty the bowls is given, only John's narrative implies any time lag.

> And I heard a great voice out of the temple saying to the seven angels, Go your ways, and pour out the vials of the wrath of God upon the earth. (Rev. 16:1)

These angel-priests hear a command to go ahead and pour their bowls out onto the earth.

> And the first went, and poured out his vial upon the earth; and there fell a noisome and grievous sore upon the men which had the mark of the beast, and upon them which worshipped his image. (Rev. 16:2)

I believe the sores are the result of an allergic reaction to the biochip I mentioned in chapter 13.

> And the second angel poured out his vial upon the sea; and it became as the blood of a dead man: and every living soul died in the sea. (Rev. 16:3)

With the second angel emptying his bowl, the seas become blood!

> And the third angel poured out his vial upon the rivers and fountains of waters; and they became blood. (Rev. 16:4)

Now, the rivers and all other sources of water are turned to blood! Humanity has wanted the blood of the saints, so God gives them only blood to drink!

> And I heard the angel of the waters say, Thou art righteous, O Lord, which art, and wast, and shalt be, because thou hast judged thus. (Rev. 16:5)

The third angel announces that God is righteous. Because the world wanted the blood of the saints and prophets, He has finally given them blood to drink!

> For they have shed the blood of saints and prophets, and thou hast given them blood to drink; for they are worthy. And I heard another out of the altar say, Even so, Lord God Almighty, true and righteous are thy judgments. (Rev. 16:6–7)

Here, another angel testifies that what the first angel said is true.

> And the fourth angel poured out his vial upon the sun; and power was given unto him to scorch men with fire. And men were scorched with great heat, and blasphemed the name of God, which hath power over these plagues: and they repented not to give him glory. (Rev. 16:8–9)

The fourth angel pours his bowl out upon the sun. Astronomers tell us that if the sun were to go nova, then this prophecy would be fulfilled.

> And the fifth angel poured out his vial upon the seat of the beast; and his kingdom was full of darkness; and they gnawed their tongues for pain, And blasphemed the God of heaven because of their pains and their sores, and repented not of their deeds. (Rev. 16:10–11)

Even though the world is racked with pain from the sun, unbelievers refuse to repent and must suffer.

> And the sixth angel poured out his vial upon the great
> river Euphrates; and the water thereof was dried up,
> that the way of the kings of the east might be prepared.
> (Rev. 16:12)

When the sixth angel pours out his bowl, the great River Euphrates dries up, making it possible for an incredible army to pass over on dry land.

> And I saw three unclean spirits like frogs *come* out of
> the mouth of the dragon, and out of the mouth of the
> beast, and out of the mouth of the false prophet. For
> they are the spirits of devils, working miracles, *which*
> go forth unto the kings of the earth and of the whole
> world, to gather them to the battle of that great day of
> God Almighty. (Rev. 16:13–14; emphasis added)

Three unclean spirits that look like frogs come out of the mouths of the dragon (Satan), the beast (antichrist), and the false prophet (the second beast). These spirits actually come out of the demons that possess the latter two.

> Behold, I come as a thief. Blessed is he that watcheth,
> and keepeth his garments, lest he walk naked, and they
> see his shame. (Rev. 16:15)

Jesus gives a warning that He is coming very soon, although He uses the expression "as a thief." Believers at this time will be able to calculate the exact day when Jesus will appear and set foot on the Mount of Olives!

Now, Jesus gathers all of the armies of the world against Jerusalem in the Valley of Megiddo or Armageddon.

> And he gathered them together into a place called in the
> Hebrew tongue Armageddon. (Rev. 16:16)

The last angel pours out his bowl unto the air itself. This prompts a great voice out of the temple of heaven, from the throne, saying it is done. The last of God's judgments are about to complete. Jesus is free to descend to the earth and take His rightful place!

The seventh angel's bowl triggers a series of events that occur in short order. John hears voices and thunders, and he sees lightning. Then on the earth, an earthquake such as never has been seen splits the city of Jerusalem into three parts. Cities all over the world collapse. God remembers the great Babylon, and His anger is especially poured out on her. Every island disappears and, even the mountains cannot be found. On top of this, God sends hailstones up to one hundred pounds apiece to strike the people who are still alive. Again, humanity is so hard-hearted against God that they still blaspheme Him.

Scientists believe that widespread use of nuclear weapons would cause hailstones of this size. Regardless, it appears that the plague of hailstones covers the entire earth.

> And the seventh angel poured out his vial into the air; and there came a great voice out of the temple of heaven, from the throne, saying, It is done. And there were voices, and thunders, and lightnings; and there was a great earthquake, such as was not since men were upon the earth, so mighty an earthquake, and so great. And the great city was divided into three parts, and the cities of the nations fell: and great Babylon came in remembrance before God, to give unto her the cup of the wine of the fierceness of his wrath. And every island fled away, and the mountains were not found. And there fell upon men a great hail out of heaven, every stone about the weight of a talent: and men blasphemed God because of the plague of the hail; for the plague thereof was exceeding great. (Rev. 16:17–21)

Note that a Hebrew talent is about seventy-five to eight pounds, and a Greek talent is about one hundred pounds.

CHAPTER 17

Babylon, the Great Harlot

This chapter may well be the hardest chapter to understand because it is loaded with symbols. I will take time to hopefully clarify the symbols used in this chapter. First, let's start with the great harlot (the King James uses the word *whore*) that sits upon many waters. Both chapter 17 and chapter 18 address this woman and city, so I will attempt to clarify over the next two chapters. As these next two chapters unfold, we will begin to understand why God hates this woman and city so much!

First, she is not a literal woman; rather, she is symbolic of a one-world religious system. Later in this chapter, we are told that Babylon is a city (both a literal city and a spiritual city, which will be named later in this chapter) where people gather together under her protection and live. Other false religions align themselves with her, so she is both a mother and a harlot. She is a mother in the sense that other false religions (New Age, Satanism, Mormonism, Islam, and astrology, to name a few) turn to her for spiritual nourishment. She is a harlot in that the world governments align themselves with her to accept her teachings and control their people by offering the people a feel-good salvation: if it feels good, do it; we'll all end up in the same place. Well, yes. False religions will one day be gathered together ... in hell and then the lake of fire. This one-world religious system will give comfort to many other false doctrines, encouraging them to reach out and offer an acceptable message to the world in general.

> And there came one of the seven angels which had the seven vials, and talked with me, saying unto me, Come hither; I will shew unto thee the judgment of the great whore that sitteth upon many waters. (Rev. 17:1)

Before I continue, I would like to address what is meant by "that sitteth upon many waters." Again, this is not meant literally but symbolically, although if one searched hard enough, one might find a literal city that sits upon many rivers.

The many waters here are symbolic of people! God considers her a harlot because she spiritually abandons the true God and the true Savior, Christ Jesus!

In the natural sense, a harlot commits fornication or adultery with men, women, and even animals. In a spiritual sense, a harlot is someone who has stopped worshipping the true God and worships anything or anyone else!

> With whom the kings of the earth have committed fornication, and the inhabitants of the earth have been made drunk with the wine of her fornication. (Rev. 17:2)

In verse 2, we learn that the kings of the earth, the government leaders, follow her false teachings and therefore have become drunk with the wine (false teachings) of her fornication. The harlot teaches peace, love, and tolerance—except when it comes to Jesus Christ. Then the harlot denies Him and teaches her daughters (false religions) to teach the same. Her sons-in-law would be any and all leaders, governments, and religions who hold to her teachings!

> So he carried me away in the spirit into the wilderness: and I saw a woman sit upon a scarlet coloured beast, full of names of blasphemy, having seven heads and ten horns. (Rev. 17:3)

Here we find that John is taken in the spirit into the wilderness (the lost world, if you will) and sees the woman sitting upon a scarlet beast full of names of blasphemy; the beast has seven heads and ten horns.

This would indicate that the woman and beast have an alliance. For now, at least, the beast lets the woman feel as though she is in control. Hence, she rides the beast. The beast itself has seven heads and ten horns, symbolizing seven main world leaders having control of ten primary governments or kingdoms.

> And the woman was arrayed in purple and scarlet colour,
> and decked with gold and precious stones and pearls,
> having a golden cup in her hand full of abominations
> and filthiness of her fornication. (Rev. 17:4)

Verse 4 gives more information about the woman. We are told she is arrayed in purple and scarlet colors, the colors of royalty. She is decked with gold and precious stone and pearls, and she has a golden cup in her hand full of the abominations and filthiness of her fornication. The cup holds the teachings or wine of demons who entice the world with false teachings and make people drunk with the same.

> And upon her forehead *was* a name written, Mystery,
> Babylon The Great, The Mother Of Harlots And
> Abominations Of The Earth. (Rev. 17:5)

In verse 5 we find out that a name is written on her forehead: "Mystery, Babylon The Great, The Mother Of Harlots And Abominations Of The Earth." This name tells us that the woman symbolizes a city and the mother of harlots and abominations. She is a city. Here, there is possibly a double reference. Scripture seems to support the idea that Babylon the Great is a literal city at the same time, telling us that Babylon the Great is a symbolic city. Spiritually, it is a birthplace of abominations and false teachings that spread out through the earth. It is literal in the sense that people can travel to the city itself and participate in any manner or number or sins that they want!

> And I saw the woman drunken with the blood of the
> saints, and with the blood of the martyrs of Jesus: and
> when I saw her, I wondered with great admiration. (Rev.
> 17:6)

Verse 6 states that John saw the woman drunk with the blood of the saints, meaning she enjoyed and derived extreme pleasure out of the sufferings and deaths of believers coming out of the tribulation.

For clarity, I will examine verses 7–12 together because these verses are so closely relate to each other.

And the angel said unto me, Wherefore didst thou marvel? I will tell thee the mystery of the woman, and of the beast that carrieth her, which hath the seven heads and ten horns. The beast that thou sawest was, and is not; and shall ascend out of the bottomless pit, and go into perdition: and they that dwell on the earth shall wonder, whose names were not written in the book of life from the foundation of the world, when they behold the beast that was, and is not, and yet is. (Rev. 17:7–8)

So I don't overload the reader with too much information at once, I'll concentrate on verses 7 and 8. Remember back in Revelation 17:1, one of the angels who had held one of the seven bowls (vials) comes over to John and talks with him. Here, the angel asks John why he marvels at the woman who sits on the seven-headed, ten-horned beast. In verse 7, the angel tells John that he will tell John the mystery of the woman and of the beast that carries her, which has seven heads and ten horns.

In verse 8, we learn more about the beast itself.

And here is the mind which hath wisdom. The seven heads are seven mountains, on which the woman sitteth. (Rev. 17:9)

Now that I have no doubt muddied the water, I shall start to clear things up. With verse 9, we learn that with wisdom, we can understand that the seven heads here are seven mountains on which the woman sits.

The only city that sits on seven mountains or hills is Vatican City; the home of the false prophet. More specifically, it is in Rome itself! Remember the old adage "When in Rome, do as the Romans do"? In this case, it means worship anything or anyone other than the true God and His Son, Jesus the Christ. If you like it and it feels good, do it. Who is going to stop you?

The world really does not want to know the answer.

And there are seven kings: five are fallen, and one is, and the other is not yet come; and when he cometh, he must continue a short space. (Rev. 17:10)

Strangely enough, many readers are puzzled by this previous verse. Readers are told that there are seven kings (better translated as kingdoms). Five are fallen (no longer in power), one is (exists now), and the other is not yet come. The five fallen kingdoms are the Assyrian, Egyptian, Babylonian, Medo-Persian, and Greek empires. The kingdom that is now would have been the Roman Empire, under the Emperor Domitian, who ruled Rome from AD 81 AD to 96. He died after trying to have the Apostle John killed by having him thrown in boiling oil; when that failed, he had John exiled to the Island of Patmos.

> And the beast that was, and is not, even he is the eighth,
> and is of the seven, and goeth into perdition. (Rev. 17:11)

The beast that was and is not is a demon that possessed the leader(s) of past kingdoms. Because the previous verse tells us that the beast was, and is not, even he is the eighth, and is of the seven; means that the demon once was free to possess humans, is held in a spiritual prison for demons at the time of John; then is free to possess humans again during the Tribulation.

> And the ten horns which thou sawest are ten kings,
> which have received no kingdom as yet; but receive
> power as kings one hour with the beast. (Rev. 17:12)

Here, we are told that the ten horns John saw are ten kings (divisions or provinces) that in John's time had not yet received their kingdoms. But when the beast again comes to power, the kings will receive power as kings for "one hour" with the beast. These kings are Gentile kings who receive power for one hour, a biblical term meaning a short time.

> These have one mind, and shall give their power and
> strength unto the beast. (Rev. 17:13)

These kings, we are told, willingly give their authority ultimately to the beast. I am among those who believe these ten kingdoms will be part of or have something to do with the European Union. These kings will essentially be the ultimate yes-men.

These shall make war with the Lamb, and the Lamb shall overcome them: for he is Lord of lords, and King of kings: and they that are with him *are* called, and chosen, and faithful. (Rev. 17:14)

These kings will make war with the Lamb, and the Lamb shall overcome them.

And he saith unto me, The waters which thou sawest, where the whore sitteth, are peoples, and multitudes, and nations, and tongues. (Rev. 17:15)

Here, waters are symbolic of people.

And the ten horns which thou sawest upon the beast, these shall hate the whore, and shall make her desolate and naked, and shall eat her flesh, and burn her with fire. (Rev. 17:16)

The hatred of the kings for the woman on the beast (the harlot) will suddenly become evident. No one will save her as these kings overthrow the woman. Not even the beast himself has any regard for her. Ironically, the next verse tells us that it was not their own idea to overthrow the harlot.

For God hath put in their hearts to fulfil his will, and to agree, and give their kingdom unto the beast, until the words of God shall be fulfilled. (Rev. 17:17)

In verse 18, we are told again that the woman John saw is that great city, rebuilt Babylon (Rome), which had ruled over the ten kingdoms and was left destroyed and naked.

And the woman which thou sawest is that great city, which reigneth over the kings of the earth. (Rev. 17:18)

CHAPTER 18

Babylon the Great City Is No More

> And after these things I saw another angel come down
> from heaven, having great power; and the earth was
> lightened with his glory. (Rev. 18:1)

John again sees a messenger (angel) coming down from heaven. This
messenger has great authority, and the earth was lit up from the
messenger's esteem or presence, which reflects the Shikinah (pronounced
Shĭ-kī-năh), glory of God.

> And he cried mightily with a strong voice, saying,
> Babylon the great is fallen, is fallen, and is become the
> habitation of devils, and the hold of every foul spirit,
> and a cage of every unclean and hateful bird. (Rev. 18:2)

The angel pronounces the fate of the fallen city. Notice the first thing is
that it became a dwelling place of demons, a haunt for every unclean spirit
(a lesser type of demon), and a haunt for every unclean bird and hated
bird. These birds would include scavenger birds such as vultures, ravens,
and eagles, any bird that normally feasts on a dead body, and Mosaic
law would have made it unclean or unsuitable for human consumption.

> For all nations have drunk of the wine of the wrath of her
> fornication, and the kings of the earth have committed
> fornication with her, and the merchants of the earth are
> waxed rich through the abundance of her delicacies.
> (Rev. 18:3)

Here, the nations (peoples) have drunk of the wine of the wrath of her whoring, the sovereigns (leaders) of the earth have committed whoring with her, and the merchants of the earth have become rich through the power of her riotous living. They suffer very heavy judgment from God.

> And I heard another voice from heaven, saying, Come out of her, my people, that ye be not partakers of her sins, and that ye receive not of her plagues. (Rev. 18:4)

Compare this to what the Lord told the Israelites through Jeremiah.

> Flee out of the midst of Babylon, and deliver every man his soul: be not cut off in her iniquity; for this is the time of the LORD'S vengeance; he will render unto her a recompense. (Jer. 51:6)

> My people, go ye out of the midst of her, and deliver ye every man his soul from the fierce anger of the LORD. (Jer. 51:45)

This previous verses have been taken out of context many times by overzealous preachers, Bible teachers, ministers, and often well-meaning Christians. Yes, it is good to call other believers out of a lifestyle that is not what God would want them to be living. Yes, it is proper to encourage someone who wants to get out of a particular sin or sins to move out of or away from that which is causing him or her to sin.

It is wrong to act and sound like that is the sole reason that this verse is in the Bible. In this verse, the angel is calling all true believers who might be physically living in rebuilt Babylon (Rome). Those who have other ties to the great city are called to cut those ties (i.e., loved ones living in the great city). Maybe a job or something else has them drawn to the city, yet they themselves are not physically living there.

> For her sins have reached unto heaven, and God hath remembered her iniquities. (Rev. 18:5)

In verse 5, we are told why judgment has come upon the great city. Elohim has grown tired of her unrighteousness and has now decreed that judgment has come to the great city.

> Reward her even as she rewarded you, and double unto her double according to her works: in the cup which she hath filled fill to her double. (Rev. 18:6)

Here, it would be accurate to say that Elohim has decreed that the Mosaic principle of an eye for an eye is being applied. See Exodus 21:24 and Deuteronomy 19:21.

> Eye for eye, tooth for tooth, hand for hand, foot for foot. (Exod. 21:24)

> And thine eye shall not pity; but life shall go for life, eye for eye, tooth for tooth, hand for hand, foot for foot. (Deut. 19:21)

> How much she hath glorified herself, and lived deliciously, so much torment and sorrow give her: for she saith in her heart, I sit a queen, and am no widow, and shall see no sorrow. (Rev. 18:7)

Notice that the heart is where God says the woman devises her ungodly attitude. Here, we are told that the great city thought so much of herself that she felt that nothing; not even God would ever touch her. The great city felt that because she sat as a sovereigness (female ruler or queen) and does not feel she is a widow. That means she does not feel she has no one to share her life (sins) with, and she would never see mourning (sadness or remorse). Notice I did not say repentance. The great city is too caught up in itself to ever repent. Because of this, God sends her plagues on her in one day. I believe this is a literal twenty-four-hour period of time. God is clearly fed up with the great city and now pronounces judgment shall be fulfilled. In verse 8, we find out that not only do her plagues come on her in one day, but so do death and mourning and scarcity of food—two of the very things she bragged she would never see. Added to this are fire, because God who judges her is mighty. God is the righteous judge and never makes a mistake when handing out judgment.

> Therefore shall her plagues come in one day, death, and mourning, and famine; and she shall be utterly burned with fire: for strong *is* the Lord God who judgeth her. And the kings of the earth, who have committed fornication and lived deliciously with her, shall bewail her, and lament for her, when they shall see the smoke of her burning. (Rev. 18:8–9)

The sovereigns of the earth would be any and all government or religious leaders, or even high-ranking merchants, who led the people astray.

> Standing afar off for the fear of her torment, saying, Alas, alas, that great city Babylon, that mighty city! for in one hour is thy judgment come. (Rev. 18:10)

Here, those same sovereigns who were not in the city when judgment struck stand afar and mourn and weep because of what they see. They have remorse but no repentance.

Verses 11–19 are best read together for the sake of a better understanding. Let's start in verse 11 and quickly summarize these nine verses before we move on.

In verse 11, we find the merchants of the earth weep and mourn over her because no one buys their merchandise anymore. In verse 12, we learn what that merchandise is: gold and silver, precious stone and pearls, fine linen and silk, all citron wood,[2] every object of ivory, and every object of most precious wood and bronze and iron and marble.

While researching Rome and the Tiber River, I discovered this:

> The Tiber was critically important to Roman trade and commerce, as ships could reach as far as 100 kilometers

---

[2] Thyine wood is a fifteenth-century English name for a wood from the tree known botanically as *Tetraclinis articulata* (syn. *Callitris quadrivalvis*, *Thuja articulata*). The name is derived from the Greek word *thuon*, "fragrant wood," or possibly *thuein*, "to sacrifice," and it was so called because it was burned in sacrifices on account of its fragrance.

(60 mi) upriver; there is evidence that it was used to ship grain from the Val Teverina as long ago as the 5th century BC. It was later used to ship stone, timber and foodstuffs to Rome.[3]

This tells us that as early as the original Roman Empire, ships sailed up the Tiber River to deliver trade goods. Therefore even modern ships would be able to travel up the Tiber River to deliver trade goods.

In verses 11–13, the merchants show remorse for the destruction of the great city, but like the kings or leaders, they show no repentance. Further, the merchants are more concerned about no one to buy their goods rather than with God's judgment on the great city.

> And the merchants of the earth shall weep and mourn over her; for no man buyeth their merchandise any more: The merchandise of gold, and silver, and precious stones, and of pearls, and fine linen, and purple, and silk, and scarlet, and all thyine wood, and all manner vessels of ivory, and all manner vessels of most precious wood, and of brass, and iron, and marble, And cinnamon, and odours, and ointments, and frankincense, and wine, and oil, and fine flour, and wheat, and beasts, and sheep, and horses, and chariots, and slaves, and souls of men. And the fruits that thy soul lusted after are departed from thee, and all things which were dainty and goodly are departed from thee, and thou shalt find them no more at all. (Rev. 18:11–14)

The merchants themselves expose their true selves.

> The merchants of these things, which were made rich by her, shall stand afar off for the fear of her torment, weeping and wailing. (Rev. 18:15)

---

[3] http://www.chacha.com/question/what-was-the-main-advantage-of-rome%27s-location-on-the-tiber-river#sthash.7ptxTbEu.dpuf.http://www.chacha.com/question/what-was-the-main-advantage-of-rome%27s-location-on-the-tiber-river.

In verses 16–17 we find that sadly, the merchants do not weep for the lost souls who lost their lives when judgment fell on the great city. They are more upset with the loss of their riches.

> And saying, Alas, alas, that great city, that was clothed in fine linen, and purple, and scarlet, and decked with gold, and precious stones, and pearls! For in one hour so great riches is come to nought. And every shipmaster, and all the company in ships, and sailors, and as many as trade by sea, stood afar off, And cried when they saw the smoke of her burning, saying, What city is like unto this great city!
>
> And they cast dust on their heads, and cried, weeping and wailing, saying, Alas, alas, that great city, wherein were made rich all that had ships in the sea by reason of her costliness! for in one hour is she made desolate.
>
> Rejoice over her, thou heaven, and ye holy apostles and prophets; for God hath avenged you on her. (Rev. 18:16–20)

We also find out that God pronounced the judgment that befell Babylon (Rome). Those saints who are living and died during the tribulation are encouraged by a holy angel that God has finally enacted His revenge on the unholy city.

> And a mighty angel took up a stone like a great millstone, and cast it into the sea, saying, Thus with violence shall that great city Babylon be thrown down, and shall be found no more at all. (Rev. 18:21)

Because the huge stone does not cause damage to or impact Babylon, this leads to the conclusion that this verse is more symbolic than literal. The city suffers great damage and is destroyed, so much so that no one can enter the city and fully recognize the city.

And the voice of harpers, and musicians, and of pipers, and trumpeters, shall be heard no more at all in thee; and no craftsman, of whatsoever craft he be, shall be found any more in thee; and the sound of a millstone shall be heard no more at all in thee. (Rev. 18:22)

The destruction is so complete that we are told that harpists, flutists, and trumpeters shall not be heard in it anymore. Further, no craftsman of any trade will be found in the city anymore—not even the sound of someone grinding flour!

And the light of a candle shall shine no more at all in thee; and the voice of the bridegroom and of the bride shall be heard no more at all in thee: for thy merchants were the great men of the earth; for by thy sorceries were all nations deceived. (Rev. 18:23)

Here, we are told the devastation is so complete because of the sins the city caused all of the nations to commit. The Hebrew uses a term, *drug sorcery*, which is the correct translation. The Greek uses the word, *pharmecia*, from which we get our word *pharmacy*. Even then, when the readers saw or heard either term, they understood the term to be a form of witchcraft, the second most detestable thing Elohim (God) hates.

And in her was found the blood of prophets, and of saints, and of all that were slain upon the earth. (Rev. 18:24)

To add to the sins of the great city, the blood of prophets and saints or believers and all the innocent who were killed on the earth is held to the great city's account.

CHAPTER 19

Jesus Returns

This chapter returns to the heavenly scene. This time, there is great joy in heaven as witnessed by John. Instead of weeping and pleading for revenge, the elders and the multitude of believers join each other in praising the Father, the Son, and the Holy Spirit because they now know that Jesus is about to depart heaven and return to the earth.

And after these things I heard a great voice of much people in heaven, saying, Alleluia; Salvation, and glory, and honour, and power, unto the Lord our God:

For true and righteous *are* his judgments: for he hath judged the great whore, which did corrupt the earth with her fornication, and hath avenged the blood of his servants at her hand.

And again they said, Alleluia. And her smoke rose up for ever and ever.

And the four and twenty elders and the four beasts fell down and worshipped God that sat on the throne, saying, Amen; Alleluia.

And a voice came out of the throne, saying, Praise our God, all ye his servants, and ye that fear him, both small and great.

And I heard as it were the voice of a great multitude, and as the voice of many waters, and as the voice of mighty thunderings, saying, Alleluia: for the Lord God omnipotent reigneth.

Let us be glad and rejoice, and give honour to him: for the marriage of the Lamb is come, and his wife hath made herself ready. (Rev. 19:1–7)

This is the event that believers have been waiting for! The Lamb of God and the believing Church are to be wed!

And to her was granted that she should be arrayed in fine linen, clean and white: for the fine linen is the righteousness of saints. (Rev. 19:8)

John is not talking about our own individual righteousness but the righteousness of Christ.

And he saith unto me, Write, Blessed are they which are called unto the marriage supper of the Lamb. And he saith unto me, These are the true sayings of God. (Rev. 19:9)

And I fell at his feet to worship him. And he said unto me, See *thou do it* not: I am thy fellowservant, and of thy brethren that have the testimony of Jesus: worship God: for the testimony of Jesus is the spirit of prophecy. (Rev. 19:10; emphasis added)

Anyone who thinks that angel worship is acceptable in God's eyes should read this verse and take note. Even the angel commands John not to do it, but to worship God alone! In Hebrews 1:14, we are reminded that the holy angels are servants sent by God to attend to those who are about to inherit deliverance.

Are they not all ministering spirits, sent forth to minister for them who shall be heirs of salvation?

And I saw heaven opened, and behold a white horse; and he that sat upon him *was* called Faithful and True, and in righteousness he doth judge and make war. (Rev. 19:11)

Now John sees the third heaven opened, and a white horse. Notice the description John gives us of Jesus.

> His eyes were as a flame of fire, and on his head were many crowns; and he had a name written, that no man knew, but he himself. (Rev. 19:12)

Only Jesus is able to understand the name written on the crown He now wears. Once He dons the crown, I believe every believer will know and understand that name.

> And having been dressed in a robe dipped in blood—and His Name is called: The Word of God. (Rev. 19:13)

Compare to John 1:1 and John 1:14.

> In the beginning was the Word, and the Word was with God, and the Word was God. (John 1:1)

> And the Word was made flesh, and dwelt among us, (and we beheld his glory, the glory as of the only begotten of the Father,) full of grace and truth. (John 1:14) [punctuation used exactly as original scriptures show].

Hebrew scholars believe that this means that Jesus was born during the Festival of Booths (or the Feast of Tabernacles).

> And the armies which were in heaven followed him upon white horses, clothed in fine linen, white and clean. (Rev. 19:14)

Notice the position of the army: "we will follow Christ." He is the one who makes war with all those on earth, including Satan and his demons. We will simply observe, not participate in this.

> And out of his mouth goeth a sharp sword, that with it he should smite the nations: and he shall rule them with a rod of iron: and he treadeth the winepress of the

fierceness and wrath of Almighty God. And he hath on his vesture and on his thigh a name written, King Of Kings, And Lord Of Lords. (Rev. 19:15–16)

Because the Hebrew words for *thigh* and *banner* are so similar, it is likely that one letter was misread and thusly mistranslated.

Compare Revelation 19:16 to Leviticus 19:28 and Exodus 28:42.

If this word was written in Hebrew, it would have been *ragel*. It's possible that the copiers of Revelation could have overlooked the small extension on the *dalet* (ד), which would have made it a *resh* (ר). If the word was *dagel*, it would have meant *banner*, which makes much more sense than *thigh*, because in the latter case, two rules are broken.

In Leviticus 19:28, the Mosaic law forbids believers to make tattoos on their bodies.

> Ye shall not make any cuttings in your flesh for the dead, nor print any marks upon you: I am the LORD.

> And there followed him a certain young man, having a linen cloth cast about his naked body; and the young men laid hold on him.

See Exodus 28:42 for more detail.

> And thou shalt make them linen breeches to cover their nakedness; from the loins even unto the thighs they shall reach.

> He shall put on the holy linen coat, and he shall have the linen breeches upon his flesh, and shall be girded with a linen girdle, and with the linen mitre shall he be attired: these are holy garments; therefore shall he wash his flesh in water, and so put them on. (Lev. 16:4)

When Revelation was copied, it would have been easy to see the Hebrew *d* (ד) as an *r* (ר) if the former was not carefully written down. As the Hebrew script developed, the *dalet* and the *resh*, especially from around 700 BC and onward, looked almost identical. It is also contrary to His dress in Revelation 1:13.

> And in the midst of the seven candlesticks one like unto the Son of man, clothed with a garment down to the foot, and girt about the paps with a golden girdle.

It also seems that Christ, when he appeared to His followers, most likely spoke Aramaic or Hebrew.

> And I saw an angel standing in the sun; and he cried with a loud voice, saying to all the fowls that fly in the midst of heaven, Come and gather yourselves together unto the supper of the great God. (Rev. 19:17)

In verses 17 and 18, a holy angel stands in the sun and cries with a loud voice to all the birds of the air (midheaven) to come and gather and feast on the dead bodies of all the enemies of God.

> That ye may eat the flesh of kings, and the flesh of captains, and the flesh of mighty men, and the flesh of horses, and of them that sit on them, and the flesh of all *men, both* free and bond, both small and great. And I saw the beast, and the kings of the earth, and their armies, gathered together to make war against him that sat on the horse, and against his army. (Rev. 19:18–19)

Now, John sees the beast (antichrist) and all of the sovereigns (leaders) of the earth, and their armies gather together to fight Jesus in His glory as the second member of the Godhead!

> And the beast was taken, and with him the false prophet that wrought miracles before him, with which he deceived them that had received the mark of the beast, and them that worshipped his image. These both were

cast alive into a lake of fire burning with brimstone.
(Rev. 19:20)

Scientists will tell you that no human will ever see the inside of a black hole! Because I believe that the bottomless pit and lake of fire are two parts of a black hole, this verse proves otherwise. See my notes in regard to the bottomless pit (chapter 9 of this study).

And the remnant were slain with the sword of him that sat upon the horse, which sword proceeded out of his mouth: and all the fowls were filled with their flesh. (Rev. 19:21)

The rest were killed not by the army following Jesus but by Him with a sword that came out of His mouth. I believe the sword is symbolic of the power Jesus wields at His very command.

CHAPTER 20

The Millennial Kingdom

And I saw an angel come down from heaven, having the key of the bottomless pit and a great chain in his hand. (Rev. 20:1)

This is the second time John sees a holy angel come down from heaven. The first time was in Revelation 10:1, where a holy angel came down from heaven to touch the earth and sea.

And I saw another mighty angel come down from heaven, clothed with a cloud: and a rainbow was upon his head, and his face was as it were the sun, and his feet as pillars of fire. (Rev. 10:1)

And he laid hold on the dragon, that old serpent, which is the Devil, and Satan, and bound him a thousand years. (Rev. 20:2)

For those who do not believe that there will be a thousand-year reign of Christ, they will have difficulty explaining this verse and the next verse.

And cast him into the bottomless pit, and shut him up, and set a seal upon him, that he should deceive the nations no more, till the thousand years should be fulfilled: and after that he must be loosed a little season. (Rev. 20:3)

During the millennial reign of Christ, the only sin that will occur will be from man's own rebellious heart. Satan will not be able to tempt people into rebelling, at least not for one thousand years.

The prophet Isaiah makes an otherwise perplexing prophecy when taken by itself. When compared to the prophecy of the millennial reign of Christ, this prophecy suddenly makes more sense.

> There shall be no more thence an infant of days, nor an old man that hath not filled his days: for the child shall die an hundred years old; but the sinner being an hundred years old shall be accursed. (Isa. 65:20)

This verse tells us that someone born during the millennium and who is killed during that time, and is aged one hundred years or less, will be thought to be an infant! Anyone who rejects Christ Jesus as Lord and Savior will die before reaching age one hundred!

For centuries, the Jewish rabbis have taught that the six days of Creation are prophetic of Adam's six-thousand-year reign of earth. At least, that is what should have happened. At the end of the six thousand years, Adam (now Christ Himself) will surrender rulership of the earth to God the Father.

> I beheld till the thrones were cast down, and the Ancient of days did sit, whose garment *was* white as snow, and the hair of his head like the pure wool: his throne *was like* the fiery flame, *and* his wheels *as* burning fire. A fiery stream issued and came forth from before him: thousand thousands ministered unto him, and ten thousand times ten thousand stood before him: the judgment was set, and the books were opened. I beheld then because of the voice of the great words which the horn spake: I beheld *even* till the beast was slain, and his body destroyed, and given to the burning flame. As concerning the rest of the beasts, they had their dominion taken away: yet their lives were prolonged for a season and time. I saw in the night visions, and, behold, *one* like the Son of man came with the clouds of heaven, and came to the Ancient of days, and they brought him near before him. And there

was given him dominion, and glory, and a kingdom, that all people, nations, and languages, should serve him: his dominion *is* an everlasting dominion, which shall not pass away, and his kingdom *that* which shall not be destroyed. (Dan. 7:9–14; emphasis added)

Jesus will give all rule and authority to His Father at the end of the millennial reign. His Father then shares authority over the earth with Jesus, because Jesus is also God.

And I saw thrones, and they sat upon them, and judgment was given unto them: and I saw the souls of them that were beheaded for the witness of Jesus, and for the word of God, and which had not worshipped the beast, neither his image, neither had received his mark upon their foreheads, or in their hands; and they lived and reigned with Christ a thousand years. But the rest of the dead lived not again until the thousand years were finished. This is the first resurrection. (Rev. 20:4–5)

In the previous two verses, we learn that those who were martyred during the tribulation period are given special thrones upon which they sit and serve as cojudges of all ungodly people who persecuted them. The reign of these tribulation saints is for one thousand years. Verse 6 reiterates this idea.

Blessed and holy *is* he that hath part in the first resurrection: on such the second death hath no power, but they shall be priests of God and of Christ, and shall reign with him a thousand years. And when the thousand years are expired, Satan shall be loosed out of his prison. (Rev. 20:6–7)

We are told that at the end of the thousand years, Satan is released from his prison and set loose upon the earth for a short time (about six months) to test the hearts of all who were born during the millennium. This is to allow for the free will of each man or woman to decide whether he or she will accept Christ Jesus or will fall victim to the lies of Satan.

> And shall go out to deceive the nations which are in the
> four quarters of the earth, Gog and Magog, to gather
> them together to battle: the number of whom is as the
> sand of the sea. (Rev. 20:8)

Gog and Magog were regions of Russia centuries ago. Satan will bring those who believe him from the north to challenge Christ one last time.

> And they came up over the breadth of the earth and
> surrounded the camp of the set-apart ones and the
> beloved city. And fire came down from Elohim out of
> the heaven and consumed them. (Rev. 20:9)

Although they surround the city of Jerusalem, Christ destroys them with fire from heaven (probably lighting).

> And the devil that deceived them was cast into the lake
> of fire and brimstone, where the beast and the false
> prophet are, and shall be tormented day and night for
> ever and ever. (Rev. 20:10)

Now, Satan is returned to the lake of fire, where the beast and the false prophet have been for one thousand years!

> And I saw a great white throne, and him that sat on it,
> from whose face the earth and the heaven fled away; and
> there was found no place for them. (Rev. 20:11)

Here, John sees a great white throne, not the judgment seat of Christ where all believers stood before to be judged as to what rewards (crowns) they would receive.

> And I saw the dead, small and great, stand before God;
> and the books were opened: and another book was
> opened, which is *the book* of life: and the dead were
> judged out of those things which were written in the
> books, according to their works. (Rev. 20:12)

John calls the unbelievers the dead. Unlike us, they have been tormented in hell for the past one thousand years! They are raised to be condemned to the lake of fire and bottomless pit for all eternity.

> And the sea gave up the dead which were in it; and death and hell delivered up the dead which were in them: and they were judged every man according to their works. (Rev. 20:13)

Even the seas give up all who died at sea, whose bodies were never found or were buried at sea, and who rejected Christ.

> And death and hell (grave) were cast into the lake of fire. This is the second death. (Rev. 20:14)

See also Revelation 2:11.

> He that hath an ear, let him hear what the Spirit saith unto the churches; He that overcometh shall not be hurt of the second death.

> Blessed and holy is he that hath part in the first resurrection: on such the second death hath no power, but they shall be priests of God and of Christ, and shall reign with him a thousand years. (Rev. 20:6)

Let's jump ahead to Revelation 21:8.

> But the fearful, and unbelieving, and the abominable, and murderers, and whoremongers, and sorcerers, and idolaters, and all liars, shall have their part in the lake which burneth with fire and brimstone: which is the second death. (Rev. 21:8)

Notice that not only are Satan, his demons, and all unbelievers thrown into the lake of fire, but death and the grave are thrown in as well. For all believers in Christ, regardless of when you lived, you will never experience death again or for the first time if you are among those who are raptured.

And whosoever was not found written in the book of life was cast into the lake of fire. (Rev. 20:15)

To put this into perspective, if you are a human being during the millennial reign, and you never accepted Christ as Lord and Savior, then your name will not be found in the Lamb's Book of Life. Your sentence is eternal death!

CHAPTER 21

Heaven and Earth Renewed

> And I saw a new heaven and a new earth: for the first heaven and the first earth were passed away; and there was no more sea. (Rev. 21:1)

The renewed heaven and renewed earth John sees are what we call outer space or the universe. The ancient Jews saw this as "second heavens." The atmosphere of the earth is called "first heavens," and the home of God is called the "third heavens."

> And I John saw the holy city, new Jerusalem, coming down from God out of heaven, prepared as a bride adorned for her husband. Rev 21:3 And I heard a great voice out of heaven saying, Behold, the tabernacle of God *is* with men, and he will dwell with them, and they shall be his people, and God himself shall be with them, *and be* their God. And God shall wipe away all tears from their eyes; and there shall be no more death, neither sorrow, nor crying, neither shall there be any more pain: for the former things are passed away. (Rev. 21:2–4; emphasis added)

Here, we are promised that no more tears will be shed. No more pain will ever be felt. Although there were probably tears shed at the judgment seat of Christ, those tears were for lost rewards. The believer's salvation is secure. If you stand before the judgment seat of Christ, you will never be cast out from His presence. You might not have more than one crown to lay at His feet, but you will be there to bow voluntarily at His feet and worship Him.

> And he that sat upon the throne said, Behold, I make all things new. And he said unto me, Write: for these words are true and faithful. (Rev. 21:5)

Here, John is told that everything is made new! I believe that when Jesus came down to set foot on earth, that began a solid twenty-four-hour transformation of the earth, beginning with the earth being returned to the pre-Fall state. In other words, the canopy was being restored, and the earth was returned to the state it was in before Adam and his wife fell!

> And he said unto me, It is done. I am Alpha and Omega, the beginning and the end. I will give unto him that is athirst of the fountain of the water of life freely. (Rev. 21:6)

Jesus promises that He is the Alpha and the Omega (Hebrew renders this as the Aleph and the Taw, the first and the last]. The former is not an accurate translation. The former translates as the beginning and the end. Jesus was there at the beginning, and He is the last or final.

> He that overcometh shall inherit all things; and I will be his God, and he shall be my son. (Rev. 21:7)

To all who are counted among the Redeemed. The Lord promises that we shall inherit all of the New Creation. Further, He promises that He will be our Elohim (God) and we shall be His Sons and Daughters.

> But the fearful (those who would not confess Jesus as Lord and Savior; probably more out of fear of what others would say), and unbelieving (the ones who never believed that Jesus is the Only Way to be saved, (those who blatantly engage in sin), and the abominable (those who engaged in wicked practices. They speak the language of Christ but do not live accordingly. They will say that they are Christians but will not openly testify

'that Jesus Christ is their personal Lord and Savior), and murderers (those who carried hatred in their hearts and minds for others), and whoremongers (those who engage in fornication [pre-marital sex, adulterers (those who engage in extra-marital affairs) and those who engage in perverted sexual relations], and sorcerers (more accurately translated 'drug-sorceries' those who engage in drug usage for "kicks" and "highs", and idolaters (those who worship or pay reverence to anyone or anything other than the Living God), and all liars (anyone who distorted the truth, deceived others, and destroyed mankind by their lies), shall have their part in the lake which burneth with fire and brimstone: which is the second death.

And there came unto me one of the seven angels which had the seven vials full of the seven last plagues, and talked with me, saying, Come hither, I will shew thee the bride, the Lamb's wife. (Rev. 21:8–9)

John is shown the Bride of Christ—all believers, from Stephen to the last man or woman or child at the time of the rapture.

And he carried me away in the spirit to a great and high mountain, and shewed me that great city, the holy Jerusalem, descending out of heaven from God. (Rev. 21:10)

From his vantage point on a high mountain, John is shown the heavenly city (New Jerusalem) coming down to rest upon the renewed earth. Prior to this (during the millennium), New Jerusalem was in orbit around the earth. Because believers will have gloried bodies that can exist in outer space, we will travel between the earth, New Jerusalem, and heaven itself at the speed of thought!

Having the glory of God: and her light *was* like unto a stone most precious, even like a jasper stone, clear as crystal; And had a wall great and high, *and* had twelve gates, and at the gates twelve angels, and names written thereon, which are *the names* of the twelve tribes of the children of Israel. (Rev. 21:11–12)

And it shall come to pass, *that* ye shall divide it by lot for an inheritance unto you, and to the strangers that sojourn among you, which shall beget children among you: and they shall be unto you as born in the country among the children of Israel; they shall have inheritance with you among the tribes of Israel. (Ezek. 47:22)

And the gates of the city *shall be* after the names of the tribes of Israel: three gates northward; one gate of Reuben, one gate of Judah, one gate of Levi. And at the east side four thousand and five hundred: and three gates; and one gate of Joseph, one gate of Benjamin, one gate of Dan. And at the south side four thousand and five hundred measures: and three gates; one gate of Simeon, one gate of Issachar, one gate of Zebulun. At the west side four thousand and five hundred, *with* their three gates; one gate of Gad, one gate of Asher, one gate of Naphtali. (Ezek. 48:31–34)

On the east three gates; on the north three gates; on the south three gates; and on the west three gates.
And the wall of the city had twelve foundations, and in them the names of the twelve apostles of the Lamb.
And he that talked with me had a golden reed to measure the city, and the gates thereof, and the wall thereof.
And the city lieth foursquare, and the length is as large as the breadth: and he measured the city with the reed, twelve thousand furlongs. The length and the breadth and the height of it are equal.
And he measured the wall thereof, an hundred *and* forty *and* four cubits, *according to* the measure of a man, that is, of the angel.
And the building of the wall of it was *of* jasper: and the city *was* pure gold, like unto clear glass.

And the foundations of the wall of the city *were* garnished with all manner of precious stones. The first foundation *was* jasper; the second, sapphire; the third, a chalcedony; the fourth, an emerald;

The fifth, sardonyx; the sixth, sardius; the seventh, chrysolite; the eighth, beryl; the ninth, a topaz; the tenth, a chrysoprasus; the eleventh, a jacinth; the twelfth, an amethyst.

And the twelve gates *were* twelve pearls; every several gate was of one pearl: and the street of the city *was* pure gold, as it were transparent glass.

And I saw no temple therein: for the Lord God Almighty and the Lamb are the temple of it.

And the city had no need of the sun, neither of the moon, to shine in it: for the glory of God did lighten it, and the Lamb *is* the light thereof.

And the nations of them which are saved shall walk in the light of it: and the kings of the earth do bring their glory and honour into it. (Rev. 21:13–24; emphasis added)

And the Gentiles shall come to thy light, and kings to the brightness of thy rising. (Isa. 60:3)

The sun shall be no more thy light by day; neither for brightness shall the moon give light unto thee: but the LORD shall be unto thee an everlasting light, and thy God thy glory. Thy sun shall no more go down; neither shall thy moon withdraw itself: for the LORD shall be thine everlasting light, and the days of thy mourning shall be ended. (Isa. 60:19–20)

And the city had no need of the sun, neither of the moon, to shine in it: for the glory of God did lighten it, and the Lamb is the light thereof. And the nations of them which are saved shall walk in the light of it: and the kings of the earth do bring their glory and honour into it. (Rev. 21:23–24)

And the gates of it shall not be shut at all by day: for there shall be no night there.
And they shall bring the glory and honour of the nations into it.
And there shall in no wise enter into it any thing that defileth, neither whatsoever worketh abomination, or maketh a lie: but they which are written in the Lamb's book of life. (Rev. 21:25–27)

For without are dogs, and sorcerers, and whoremongers, and murderers, and idolaters, and whosoever loveth and maketh a lie. (Rev. 22:15)

And for this cause God shall send them strong delusion, that they should believe a lie. (2 Thess. 2:11)

Wherefore I gave them also statutes that were not good, and judgments whereby they should not live. (Ezek. 20:25)

And Jesus said, For judgment I am come into this world, that they which see not might see; and that they which see might be made blind. (John 9:39)

He hath blinded their eyes, and hardened their heart; that they should not see with their eyes, nor understand with their heart, and be converted, and I should heal them. (John 12:40)

Then God turned, and gave them up to worship the host of heaven; as it is written in the book of the prophets, O ye house of Israel, have ye offered to me slain beasts and sacrifices by the space of forty years in the wilderness? (Acts 7:42)

Wherefore God also gave them up to uncleanness through the lusts of their own hearts, to dishonour their own bodies between themselves: Who changed the truth of God into a lie, and worshipped and served the creature more than the Creator, who is blessed for ever. Amen. For this cause God gave them up unto vile affections: for even their women did change the natural use into that which is against nature: And likewise also the men, leaving the natural use of the woman, burned in their lust one toward another; men with men working that which is unseemly, and receiving in themselves that recompence of their error which was meet. And even as they did not like to retain God in *their* knowledge, God gave them over to a reprobate mind, to do those things which are not convenient. (Rom. 1:24–28)

CHAPTER 22

Jesus Reigns in Heaven and on Earth

> And he shewed me a pure river of water of life, clear as crystal, proceeding out of the throne of God and of the Lamb. (Rev. 22:1)

John now sees a river flowing from the throne of Elohim (God the Father and from the Lamb). This river is a river of water of life, meaning all who drink from it will never thirst.

> In the midst of the street of it, and on either side of the river, was there the tree of life, which bare twelve manner of fruits, and yielded her fruit every month: and the leaves of the tree were for the healing of the nations. (Rev. 22:2)

Imagine! Not only will we see the Tree of Life again, but each month it will produce a different fruit! Those who live during the millennium will use its leaves for health and healing.

> And there shall be no more curse: but the throne of God and of the Lamb shall be in it; and his servants shall serve him. (Rev. 22:3)

Refer to the curse spoken to Adam in Genesis.

> And unto Adam he said, Because thou hast hearkened unto the voice of thy wife, and hast eaten of the tree, of

which I commanded thee, saying, Thou shalt not eat of it: cursed is the ground for thy sake; in sorrow shalt thou eat of it all the days of thy life; Thorns also and thistles shall it bring forth to thee; and thou shalt eat the herb of the field; "By the sweat of your face you are to eat bread until you return to the ground, for out of it you were taken. For dust you are, and to dust you return." (Gen. 3:17–19)

And they shall see his face; and his name shall be in their foreheads. (Rev. 22:4)

Now, we are told that everyone will see God's face and Jesus's face! Because only those who believed in Jesus will be there, we are said to have His name upon our foreheads.

And there shall be no night there; and they need no candle, neither light of the sun; for the Lord God giveth them light: and they shall reign for ever and ever. (Rev. 22:5)

When the canopy was originally around the earth. Scholars believe that although there was evening (twilight), there was no darkness as we know it now. Here, we are promised that never again we will see or experience darkness.

And he said unto me, These sayings are faithful and true: and the Lord God of the holy prophets sent his angel to shew unto his servants the things which must shortly be done. (Rev. 22:6)

Here, John hears a statement from Jesus Himself! He tells John that His Father sent Him to tell His prophets and His people what must come about.

Behold, I come quickly: blessed *is* he that keepeth the sayings of the prophecy of this book. (Rev. 22:7)

Although it has been over two thousand years since Jesus ascended back into heaven, He promises that not only is He returning, but He will restore everything!

And I John saw these things, and heard them. And when I had heard and seen, I fell down to worship before the feet of the angel which shewed me these things. Then saith he unto me, See thou do it not: for I am thy fellowservant, and of thy brethren the prophets, and of them which keep the sayings of this book: worship God. (Rev. 22:8–9)

This is the second time John mistakenly falls down to worship an angel. The first time was in Revelation 19:10. At least the grace of Jesus Christ allows John to make a mistake and still receive forgiveness.

And he saith unto me, Seal not the sayings of the prophecy of this book: for the time is at hand. (Rev. 22:10)

John is clearly told not to remain silent about what he saw and heard. Except for the seven thunders, which John was told not to reveal what they said, everything else is to be recorded and shared with all who would read or hear this.

He that is unjust, let him be unjust still: and he which is filthy, let him be filthy still: and he that is righteous, let him be righteous still: and he that is holy, let him be holy still. (Rev. 22:11)

The previous verse is directed at both the ungodly (unbelievers) and to the godly (believers). Both are told to continue doing what they are doing. It offers condemnation for the ungodly and praise and reward for the godly.

And, behold, I come quickly; and my reward *is* with me, to give every man according as his work shall be. (Rev. 22:12)

For the Son of man shall come in the glory of his Father with his angels; and then he shall reward every man according to his works. (Matt 16:27)

And shall come forth; they that have done good, unto the resurrection of life; and they that have done evil, unto the resurrection of damnation. (John 5:29)

I am Alpha and Omega, the beginning and the end, the first and the last. Blessed are they that do his commandments, that they may have right to the tree of life, and may enter in through the gates into the city. (Rev. 22:13–14)

And he said unto him, Why callest thou me good? there is none good but one, that is, God: but if thou wilt enter into life, keep the commandments. (Matt. 19:17)

The previous verses are restatements of the same thing. Matthew 18:17 was originally spoken by Jesus while He was on earth the first time.

Revelation 22:14 is a restatement of Matthew 18:17. The Ante-Nicene Fathers, Tertullian (AD 208) and Cyprian (AD 251), were to have quoted these verses.

Ante-Nicene simply means "before Nicea," or before the Council of Nicea in AD 325. Nicea (a city in what is now Iznik, in Turkey) was a the location of a Christian council held in AD 325. This council established much of the current Christian doctrine still used today. The Nicene Creed has been normative for the Catholic Church, the Eastern Orthodox Church, the Church of the East, the Oriental Orthodox churches, the Anglican Communion, and the great majority of Protestant denominations. It forms the mainstream definition of Christianity itself in Nicene Christianity.

For without are dogs, and sorcerers, and whoremongers, and murderers, and idolaters, and whosoever loveth and maketh a lie. (Rev. 22:15)

And there shall in no wise enter into it any thing that defileth, neither whatsoever worketh abomination, or maketh a lie: but they which are written in the Lamb's book of life. (Rev. 21:27)

And for this cause God shall send them strong delusion, that they should believe a lie. (2. Thess. 2:11)

Here, John is told that no one who blatantly practices sin will be allowed into the heavenly city or the new Earth.

> I Jesus have sent mine angel to testify unto you these
> things in the churches. I am the root and the offspring
> of David, and the bright and morning star. (Rev. 22:16)

God the Father has sent Jesus to tell John and us everything that must happen before all sin is wiped away and we will know everlasting happiness.

> And the Spirit and the bride say, Come. And let him that
> heareth say, Come. And let him that is athirst come.
> And whosoever will, let him take the water of life freely.
> (Rev. 22:17)

Both the Holy Spirit and the Bride of Christ call to everyone. Although many will reject this call, those who answer will be given the water of life free of charge. Jesus already paid the price, and He chooses to give it to anyone who believes.

> For I testify unto every man that heareth the words of
> the prophecy of this book, If any man shall add unto
> these things, God shall add unto him the plagues that
> are written in this book. (Rev. 22:18)

If anyone adds to them, God shall add to him the plagues that are written in this book.

> And if any man shall take away from the words of the
> book of this prophecy, God shall take away his part out
> of the book of life, and out of the holy city, and from the
> things which are written in this book. (Rev. 22:19)

In verses 18 and 19, we are told that if anyone adds to this prophecy (meaning someone deliberately teaches something that is not there), God will add to him or her the plagues and shall take away rewards that are written in this book.

He which testifieth these things saith, Surely I come quickly. Amen. Even so, come, Lord Jesus. (Rev. 22:20)

Even though it has been over two thousand years, Jesus points out that He is coming very soon and to be ready.

The grace of our Lord Jesus Christ be with you all. Amen. (Rev. 22:21)

In Genesis 1:3, God said, "Let there be light." Now we hear "Amen" or "Let it be so."

BIBLIOGRAPHY

Halley, Henry H. *Halley's Bible Handbook.* Zondervan Publishing House, 1965.

http://www.catholic-pages.com/grabbag/malachy.asp. www.catholic-pages.com

http://malachyprophecy.com.

http://www.biblestudytools.com/history/early-church-fathers/ante-nicene.

http://cappadocia-elenatruva.ru/iznik-dobratsya-karta-oteli-pokupki.html.

http://www.worldatlas.com/webimage/countrys/asia/tr.htm.

Printed in the United States
By Bookmasters